THE EXQUISITE COLORING BOOK

Book 1

MANDALA
LACES
GEOMETRIC &
TESSELLATE PATTERNS

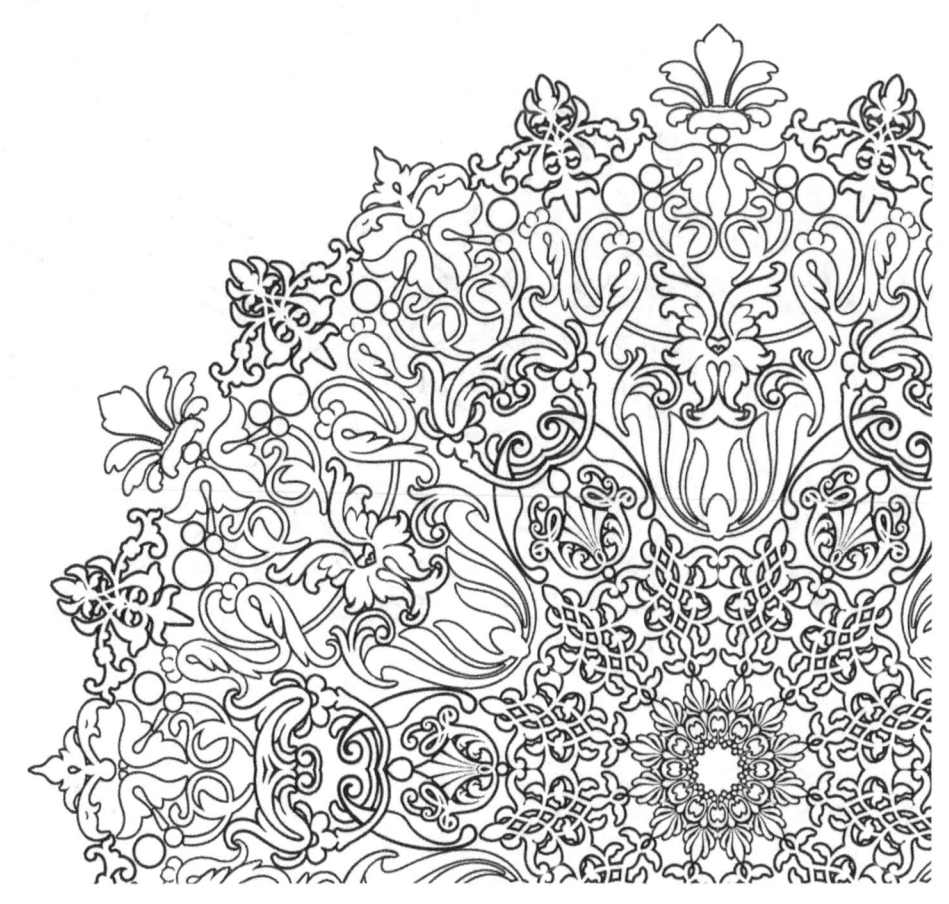

Preface

The Exquisite Coloring Book series is one of the most enjoyable and attracting adult coloring books for all age groups. This is the ideal place to translate your mind ideas into beautiful colorful designs. This is the **book 1** in **The Exquisite Coloring Book** series which contains 50 unique shapes including beautiful laces, mandala, geometric and tessellated patterns. All shapes are the products of complex steps of hand drawing merged with digital manipulation to optimize lines and symmetry. We hope these little pieces of art will help you release from stress with each stroke of your colored pen, and sharpen your creative edge. All you need is a set of colored pens or pencils to have great fun.

A. Fouda
M. Qutb

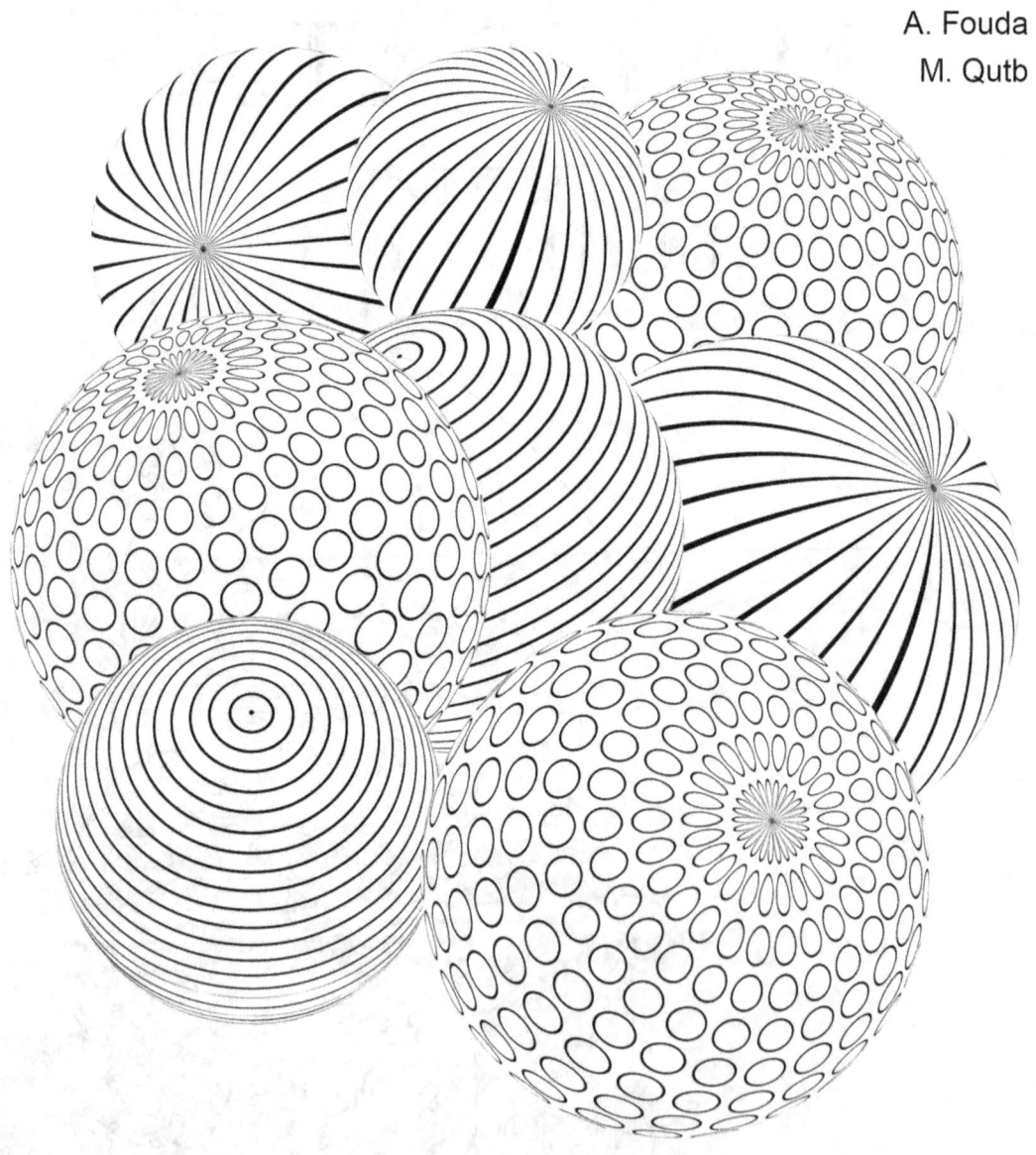

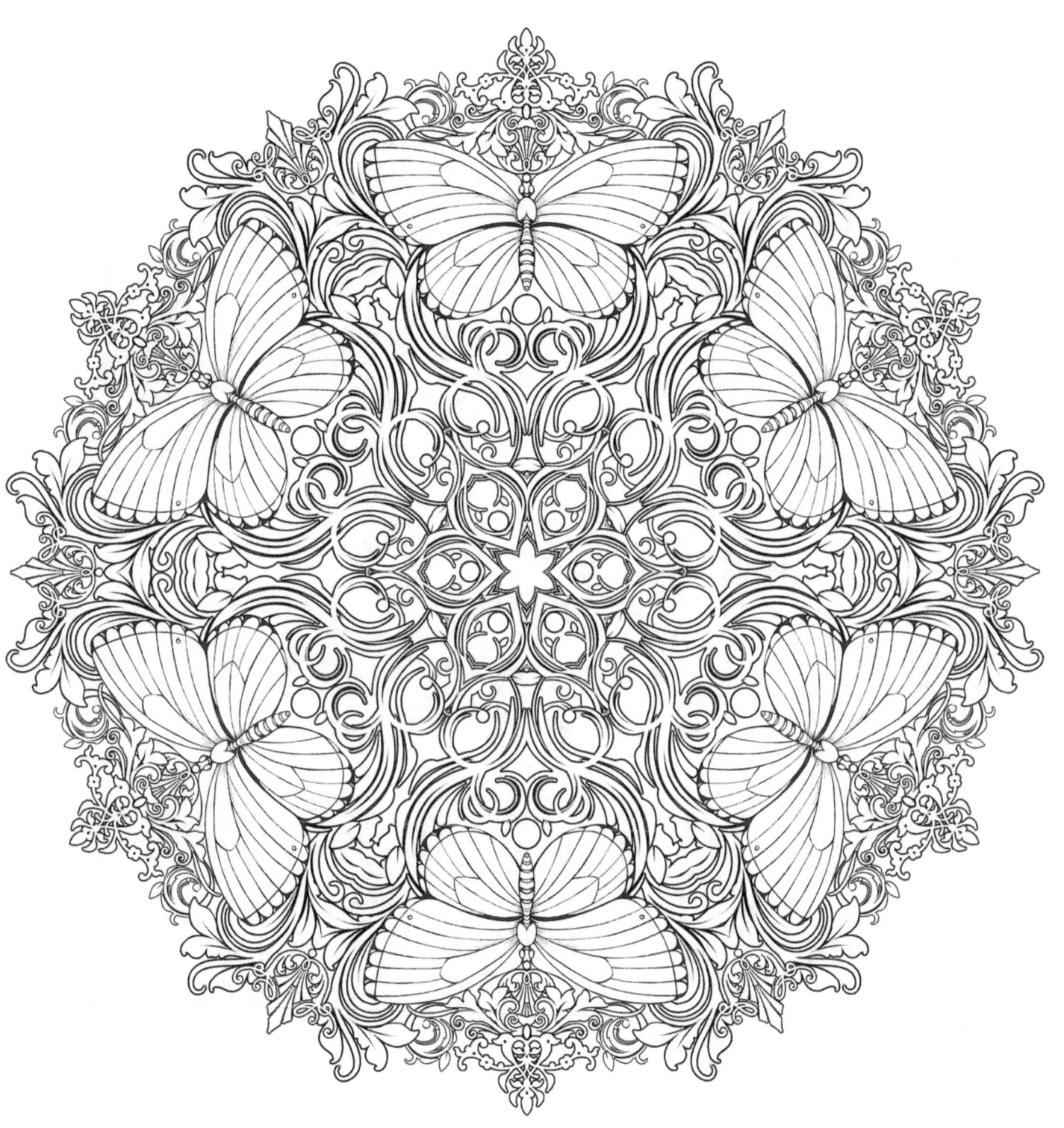

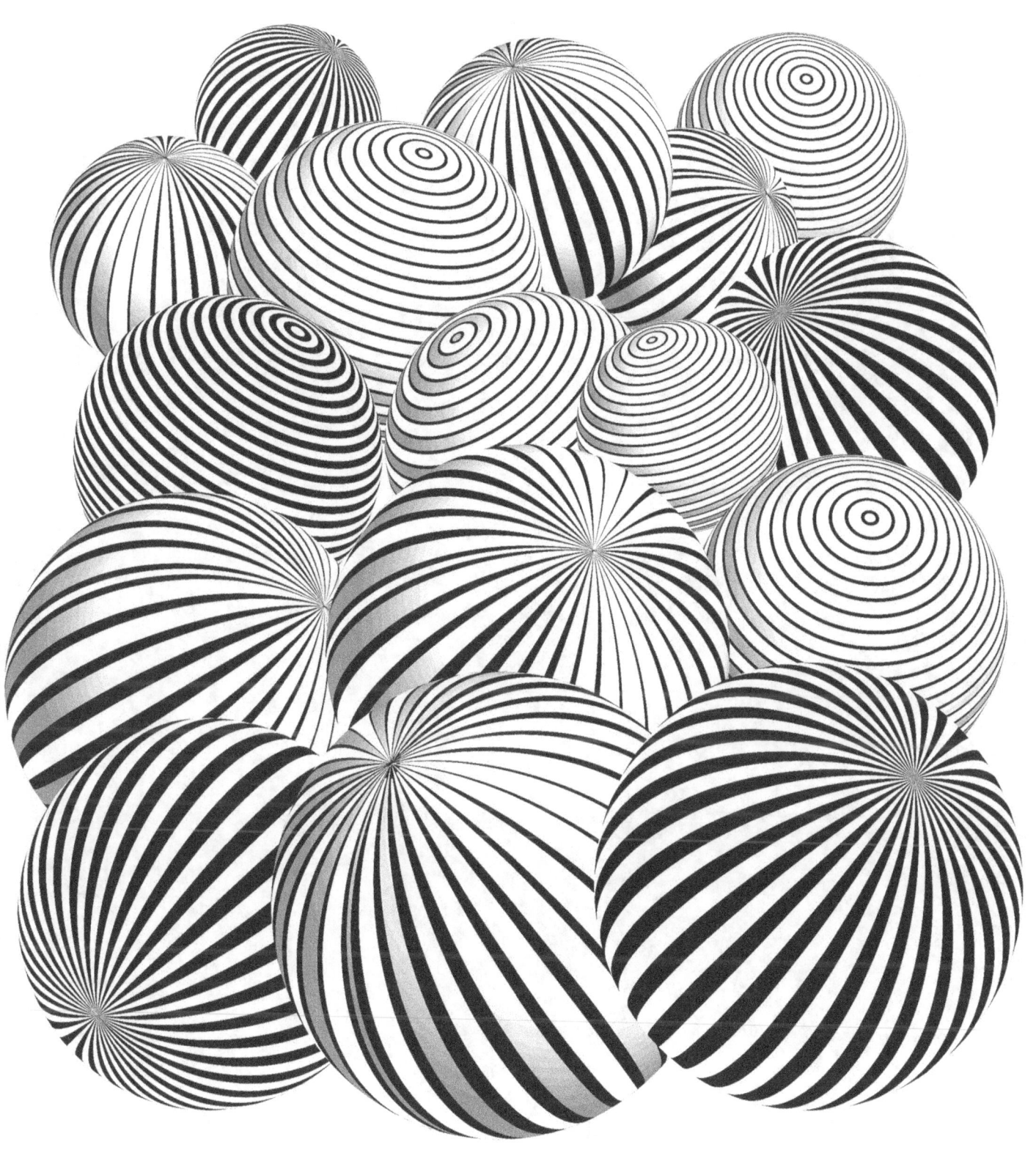

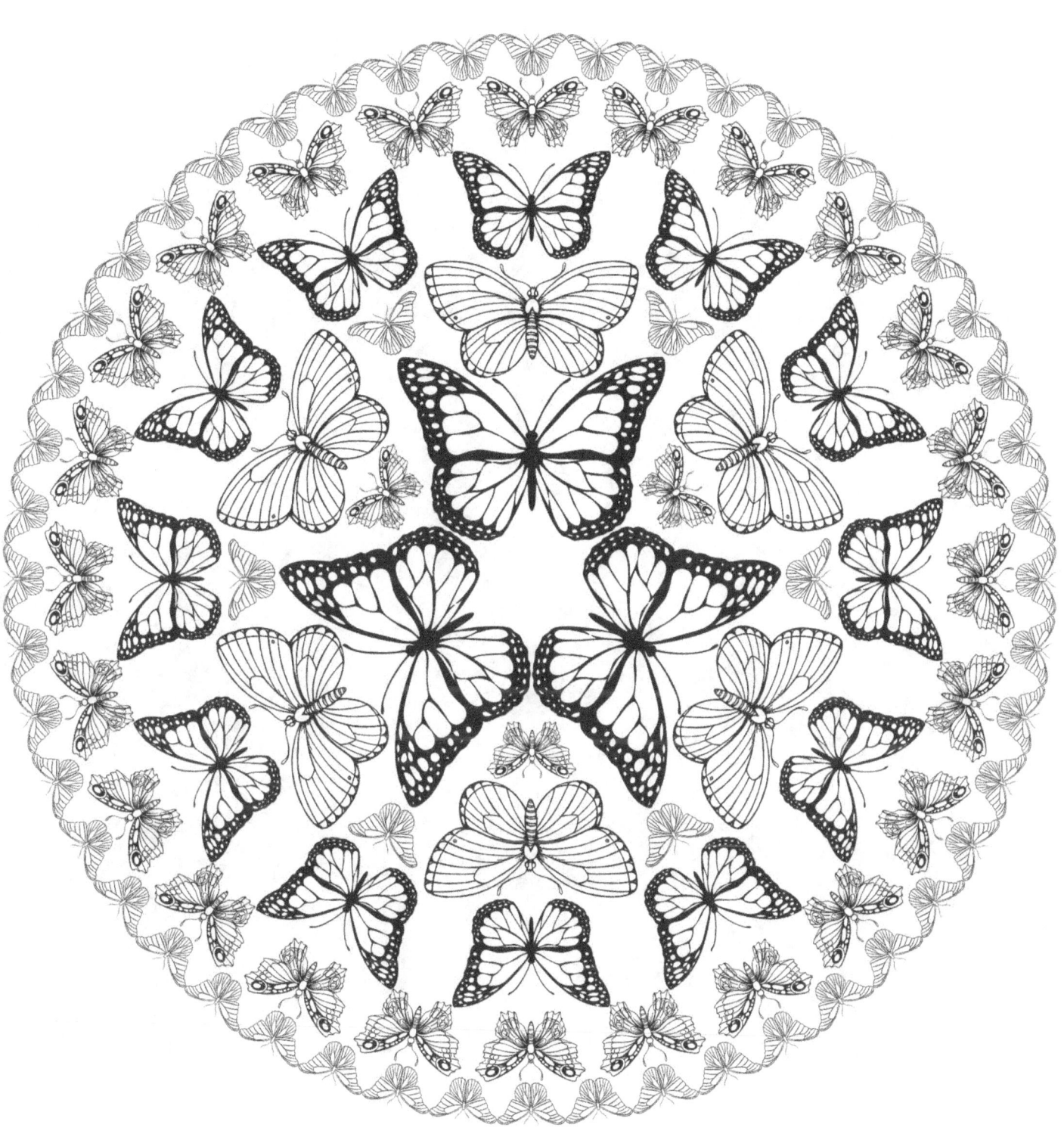

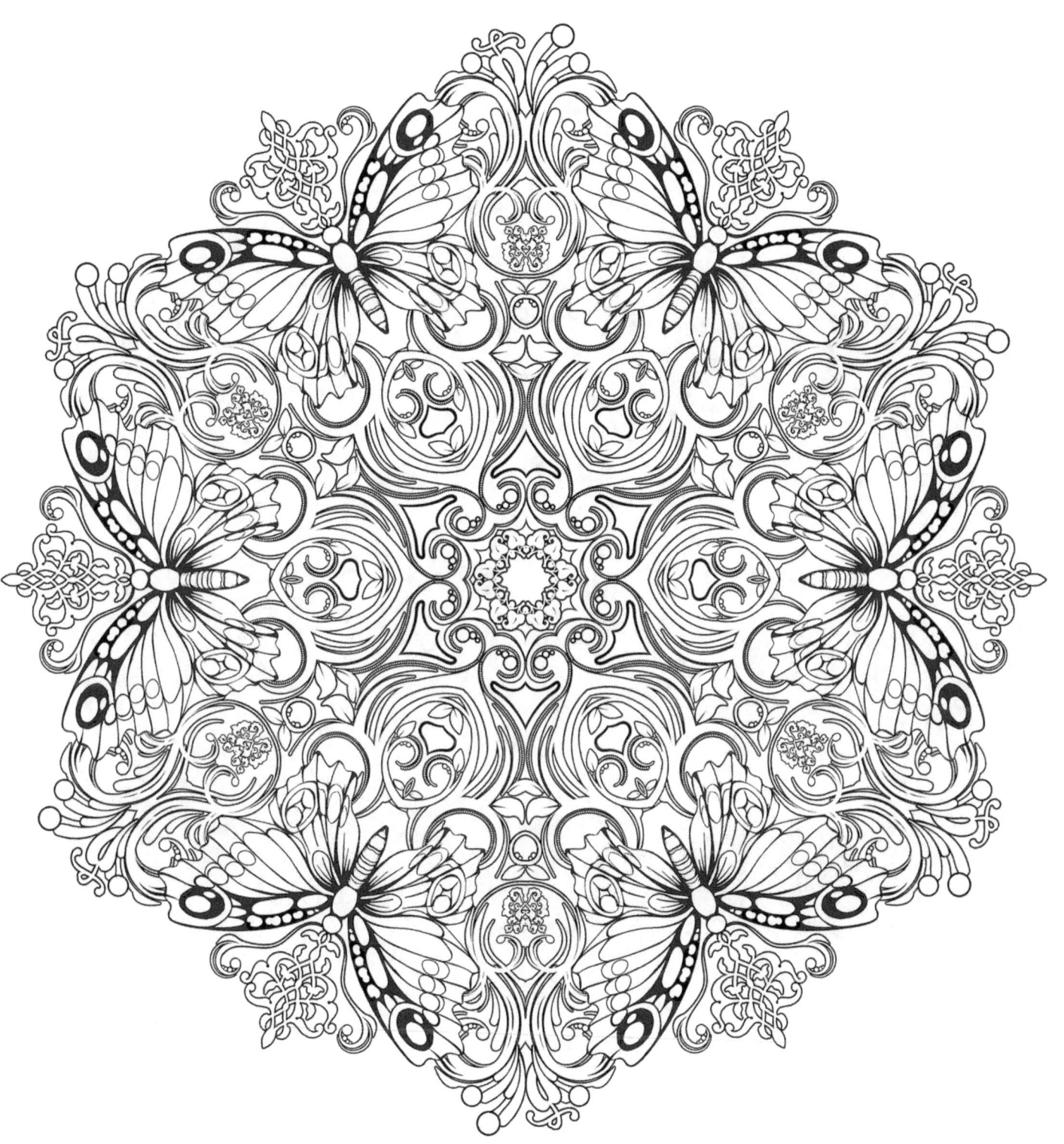

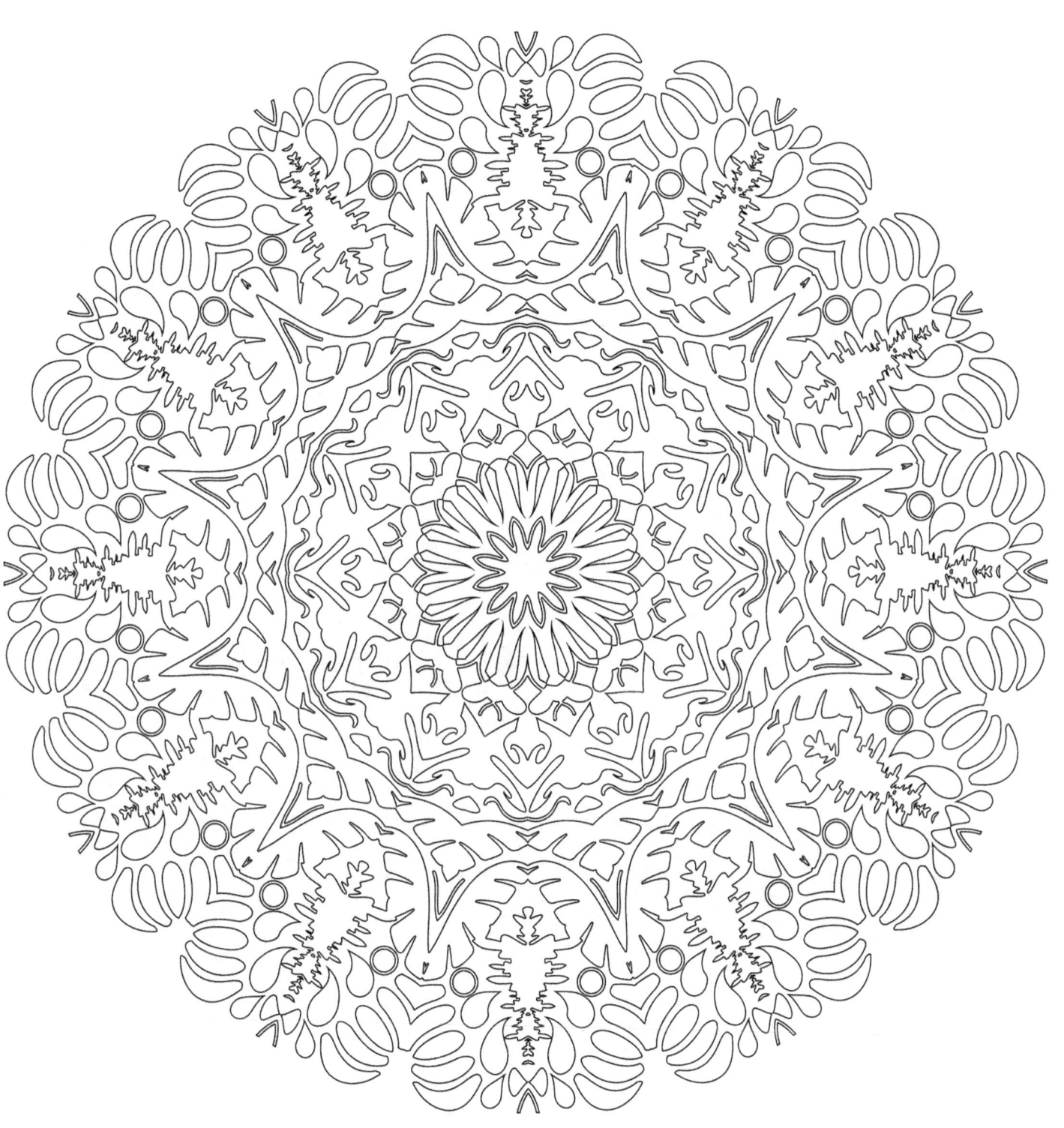

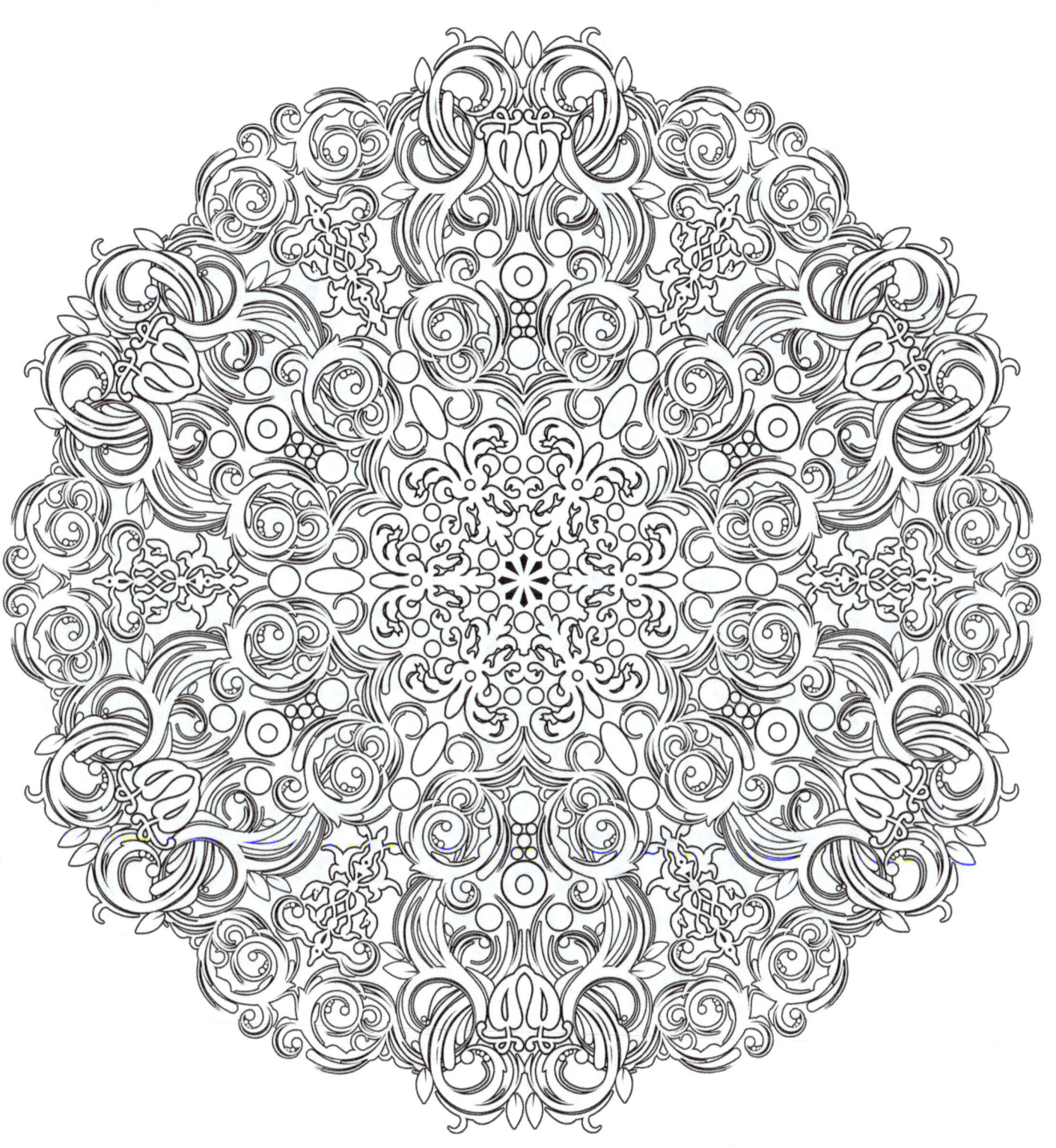

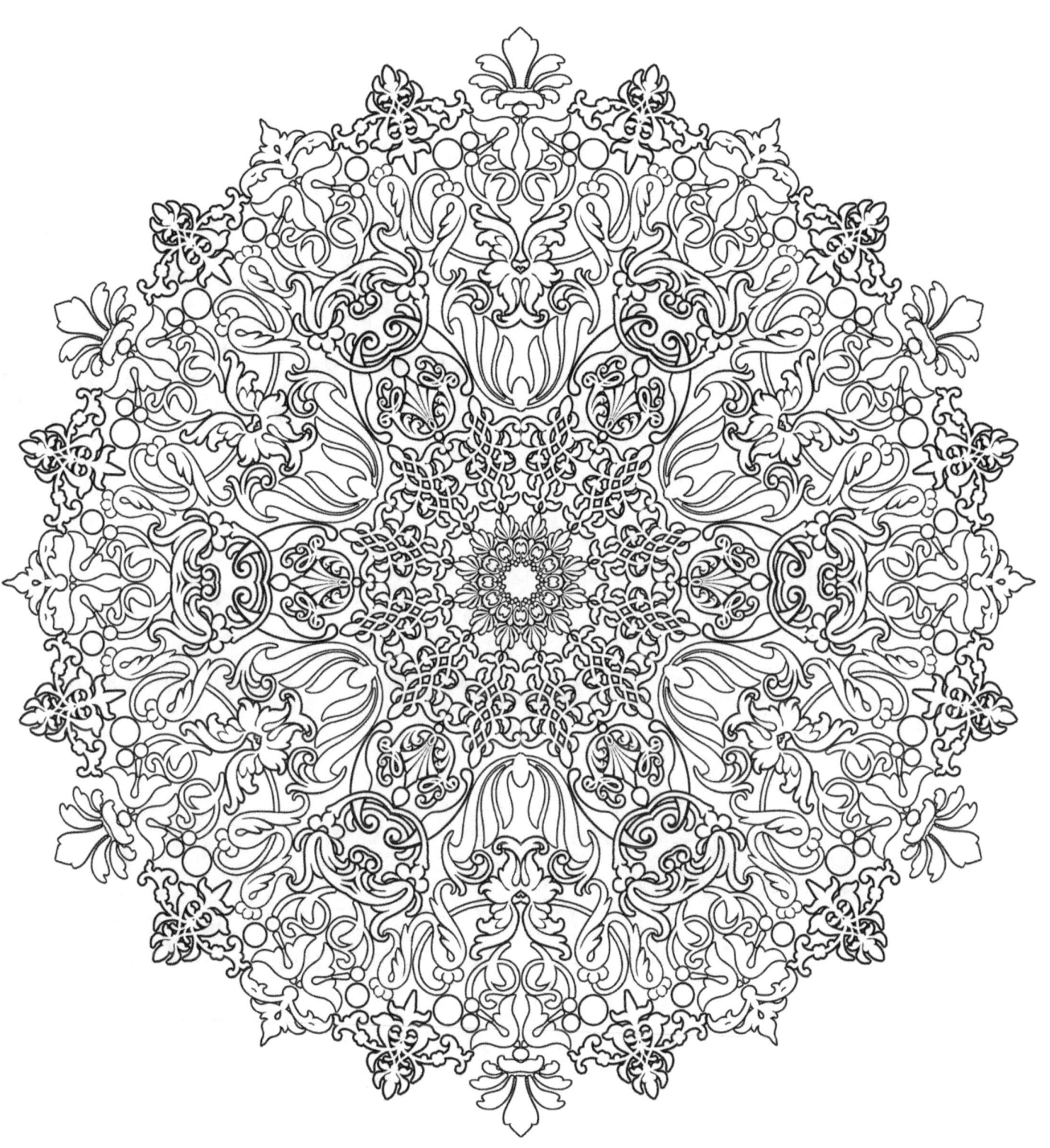

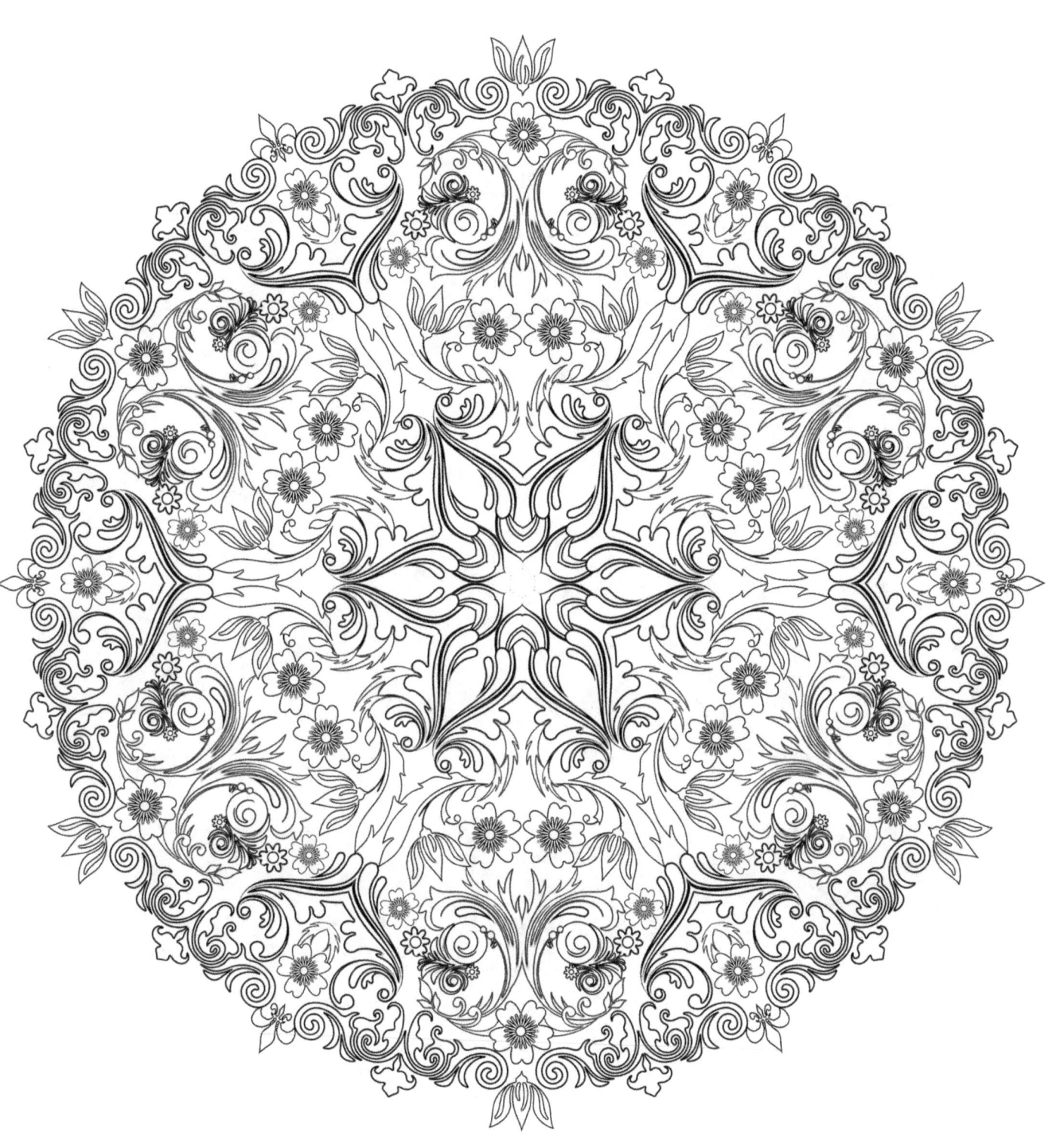

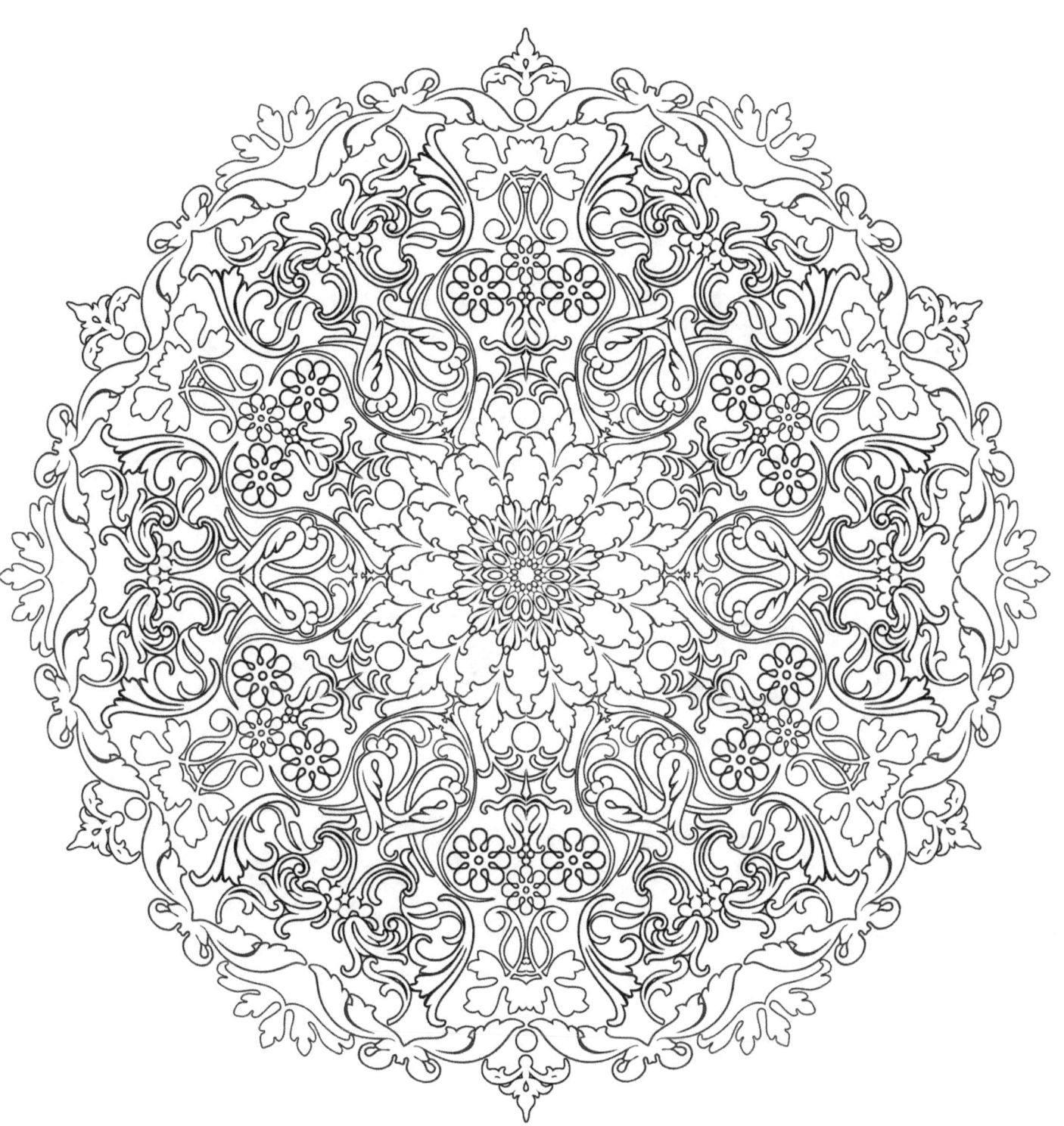

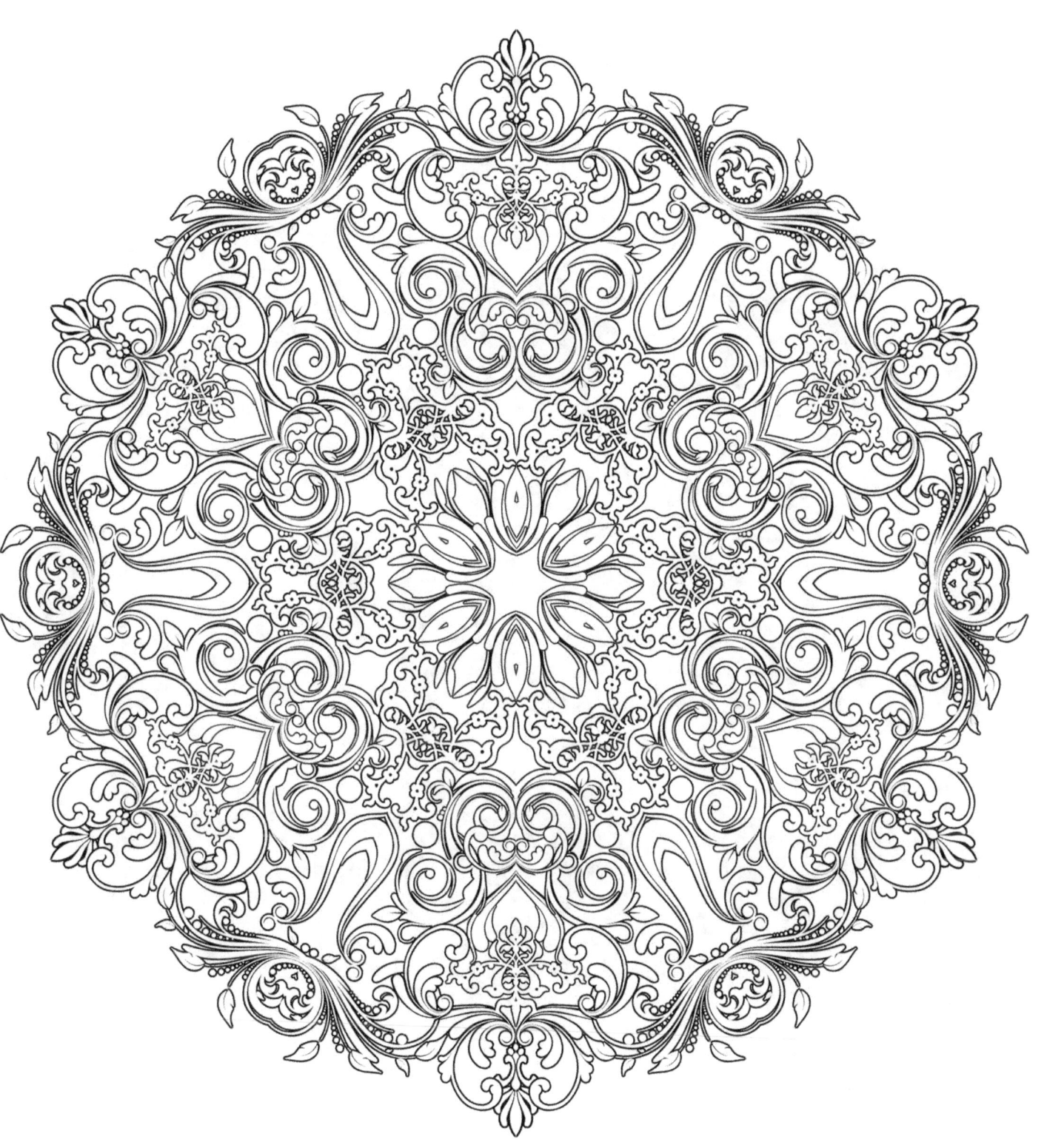

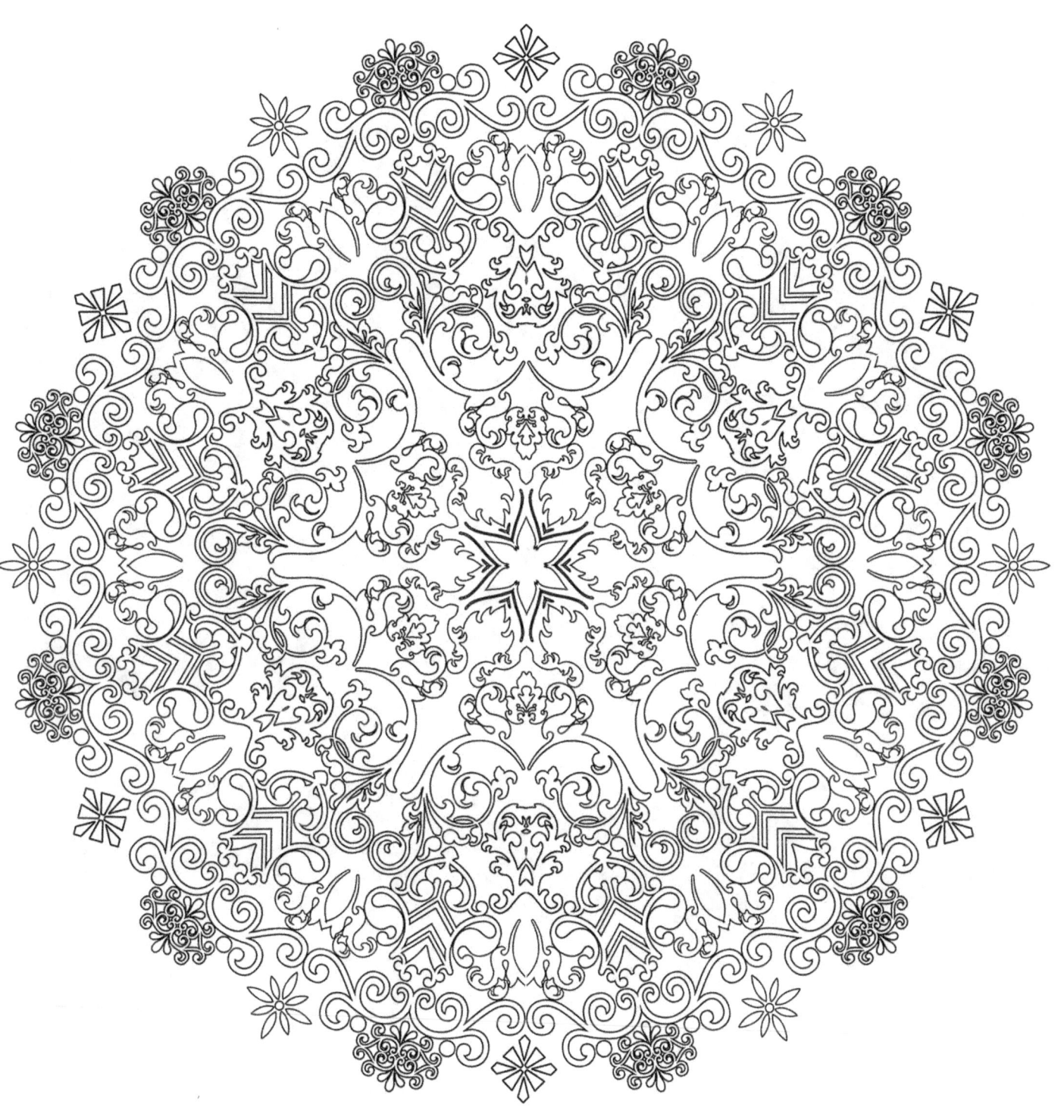

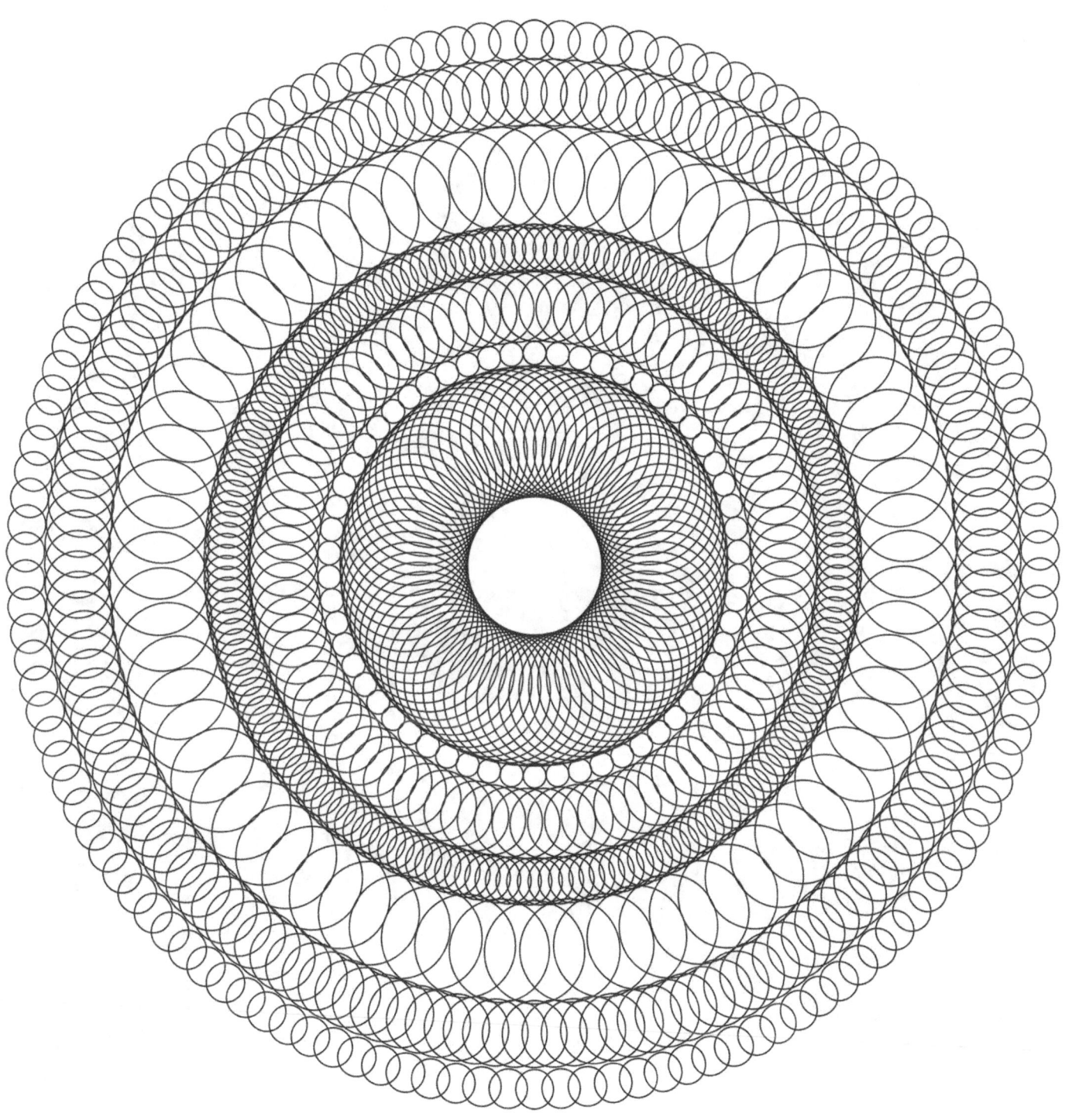

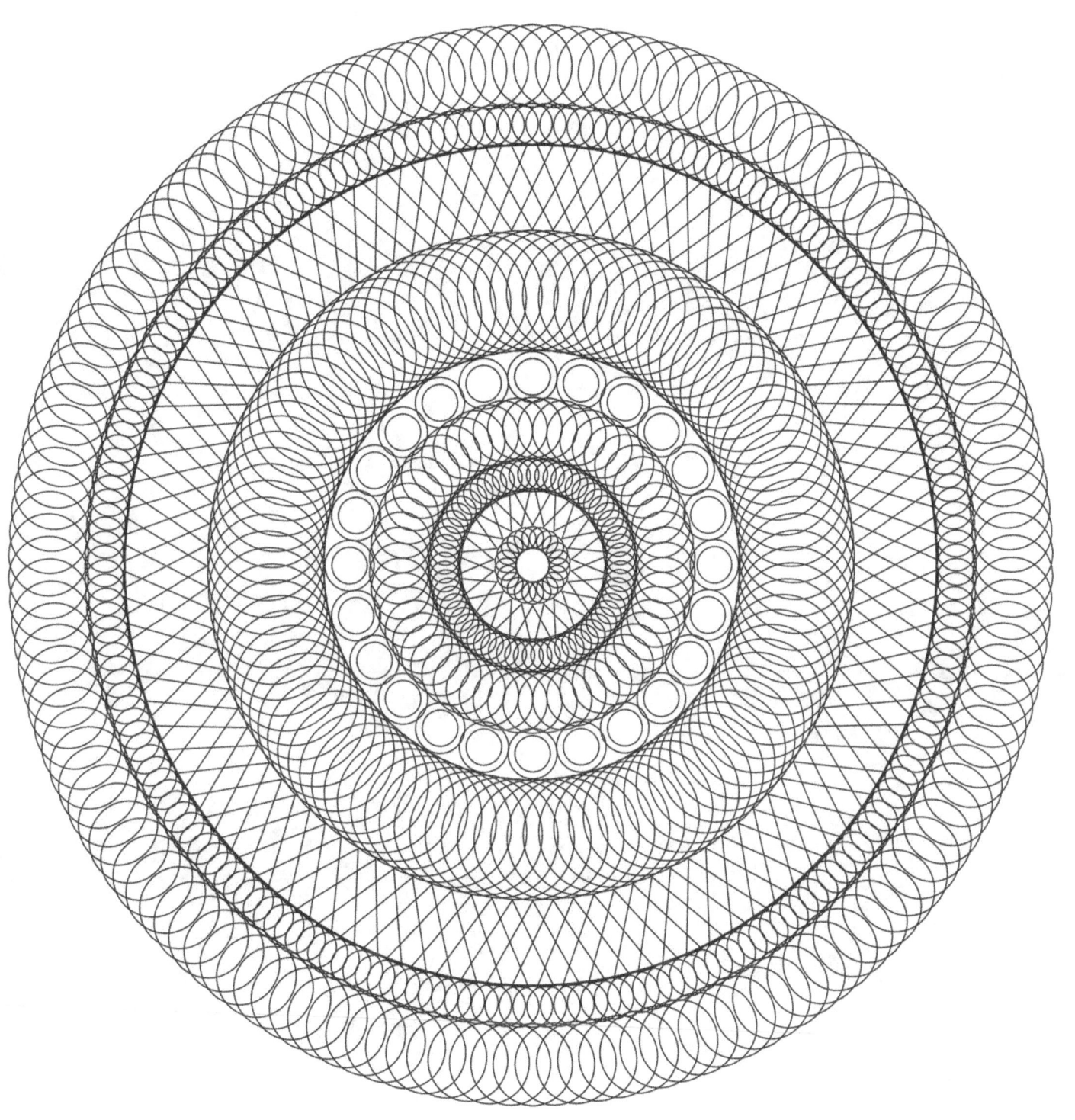

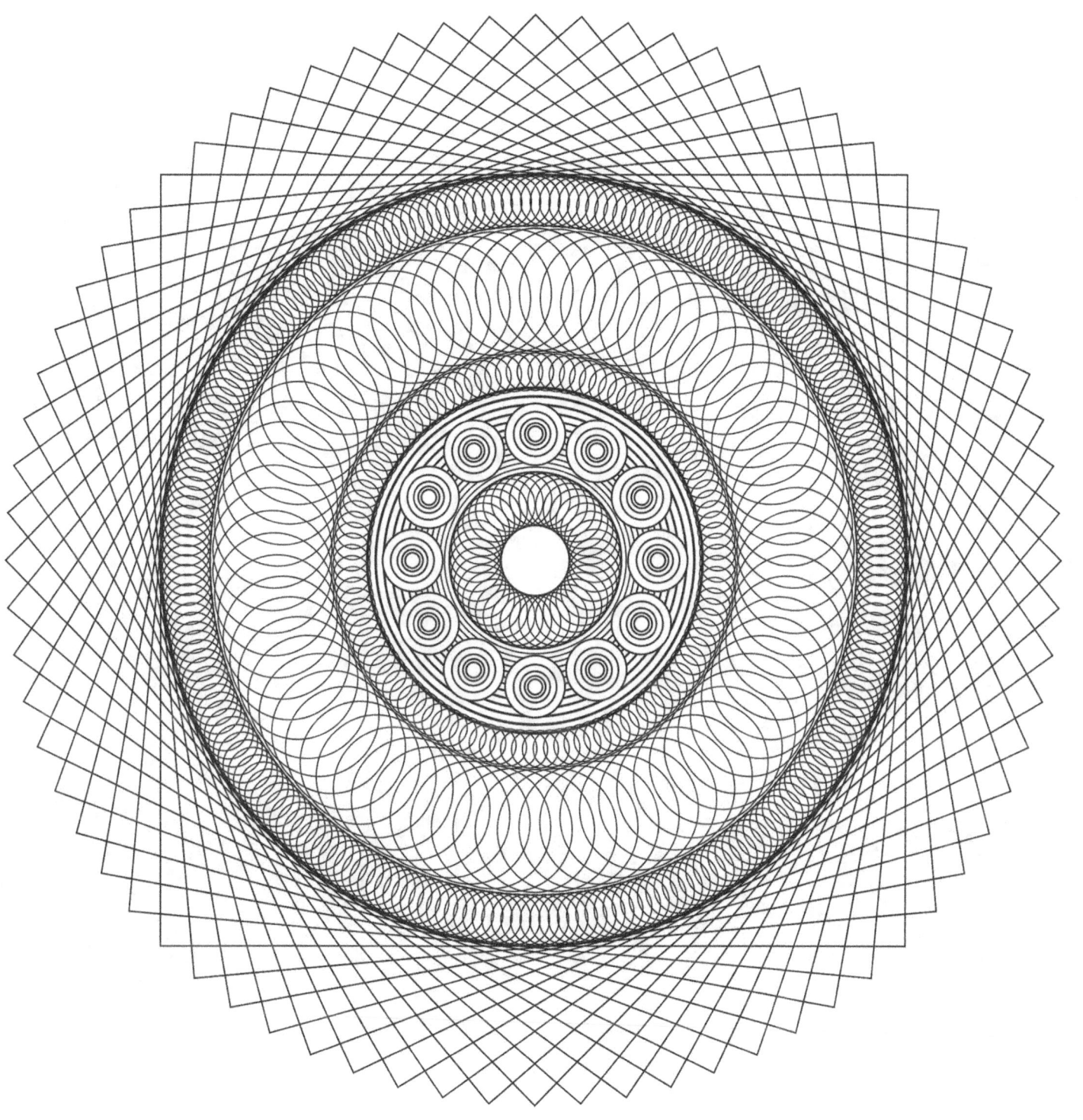

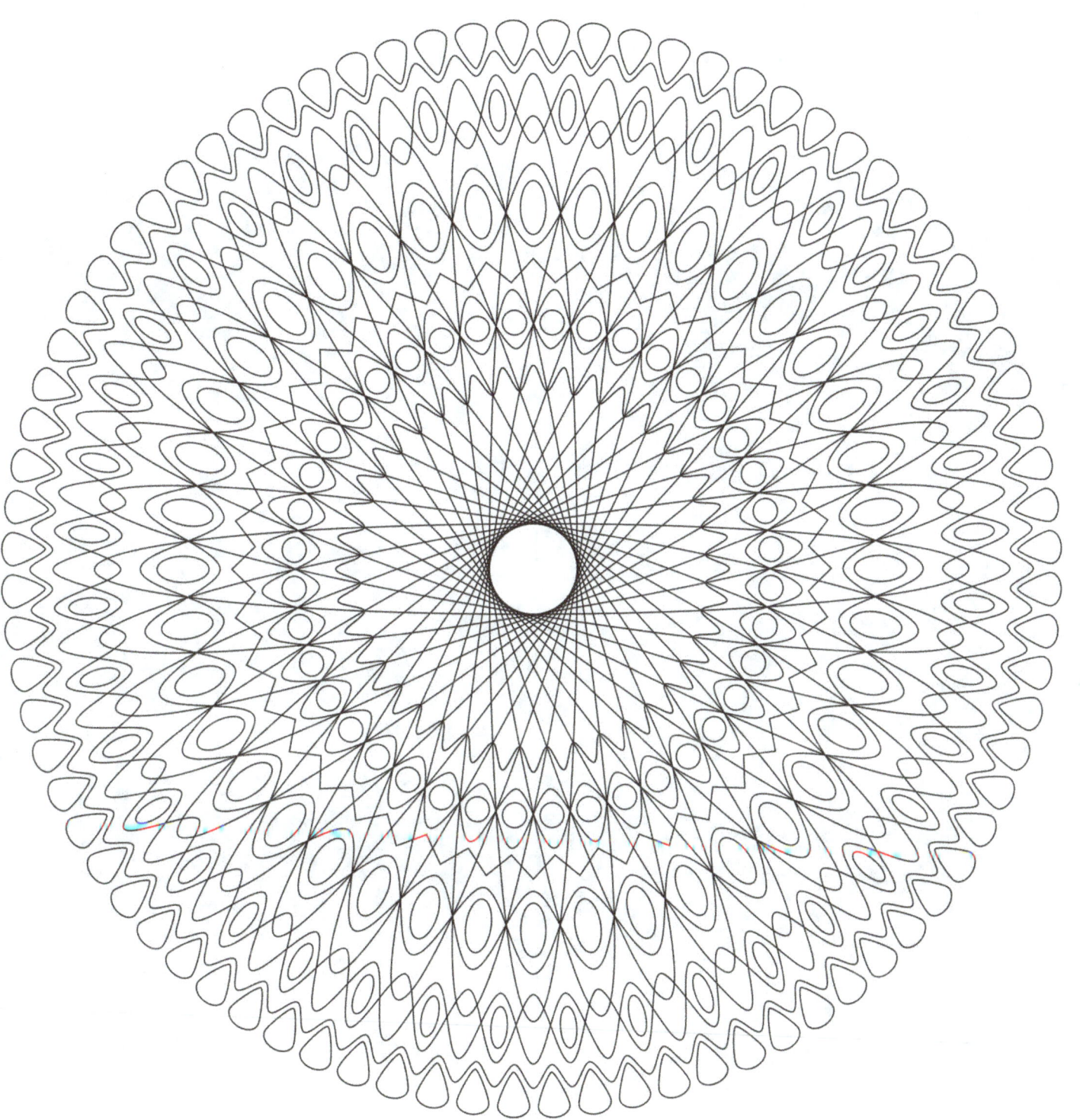

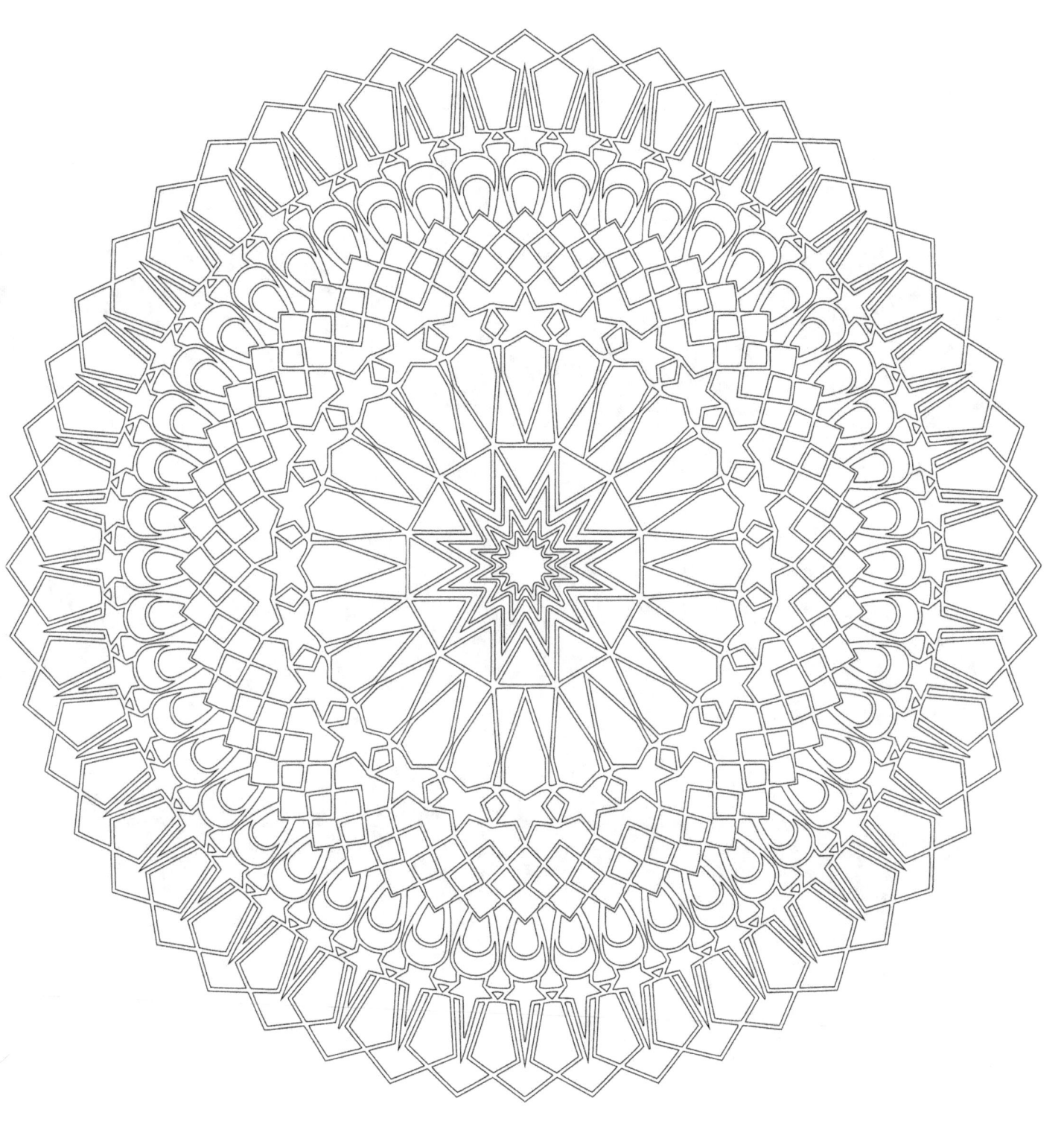

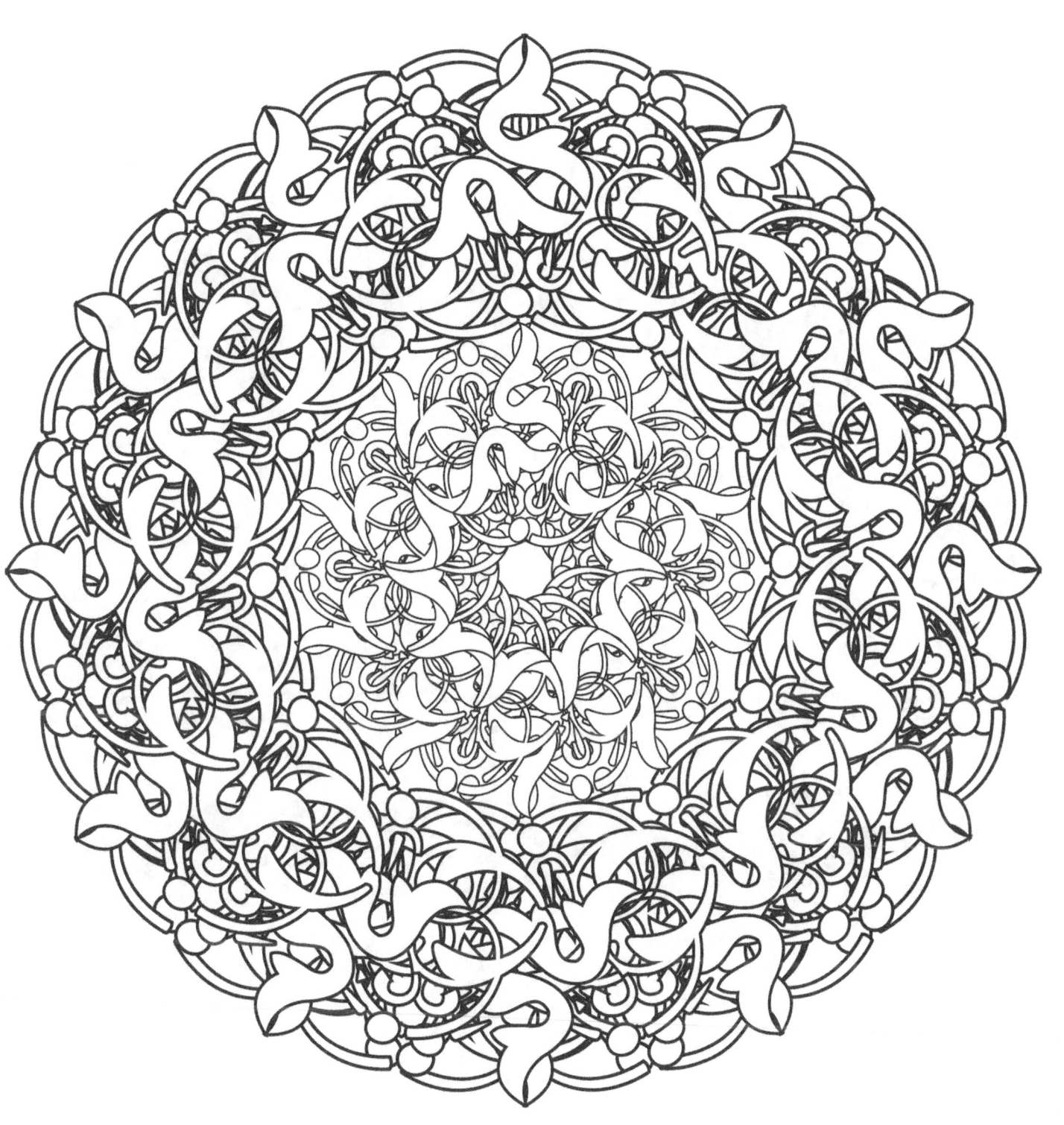

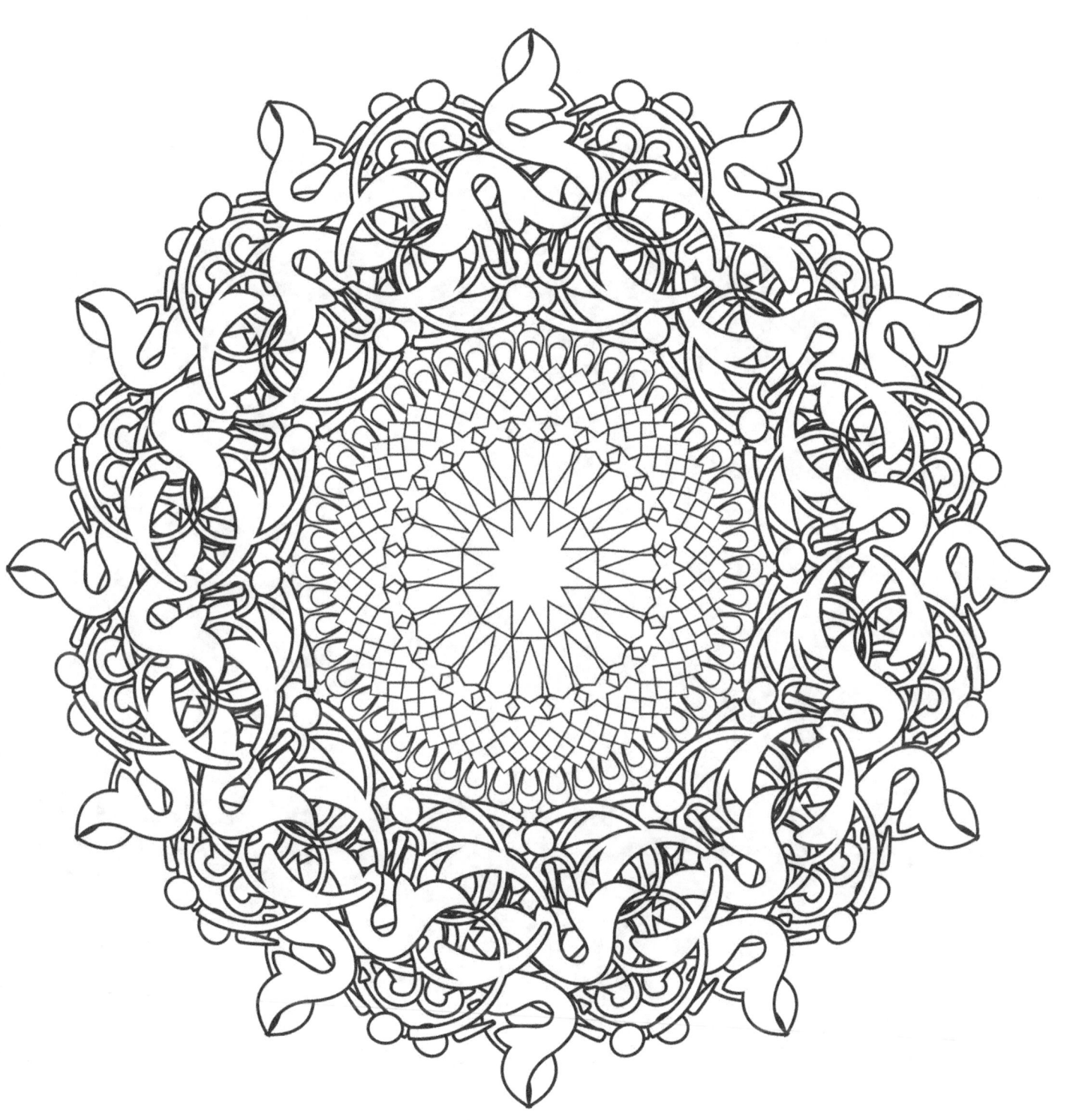

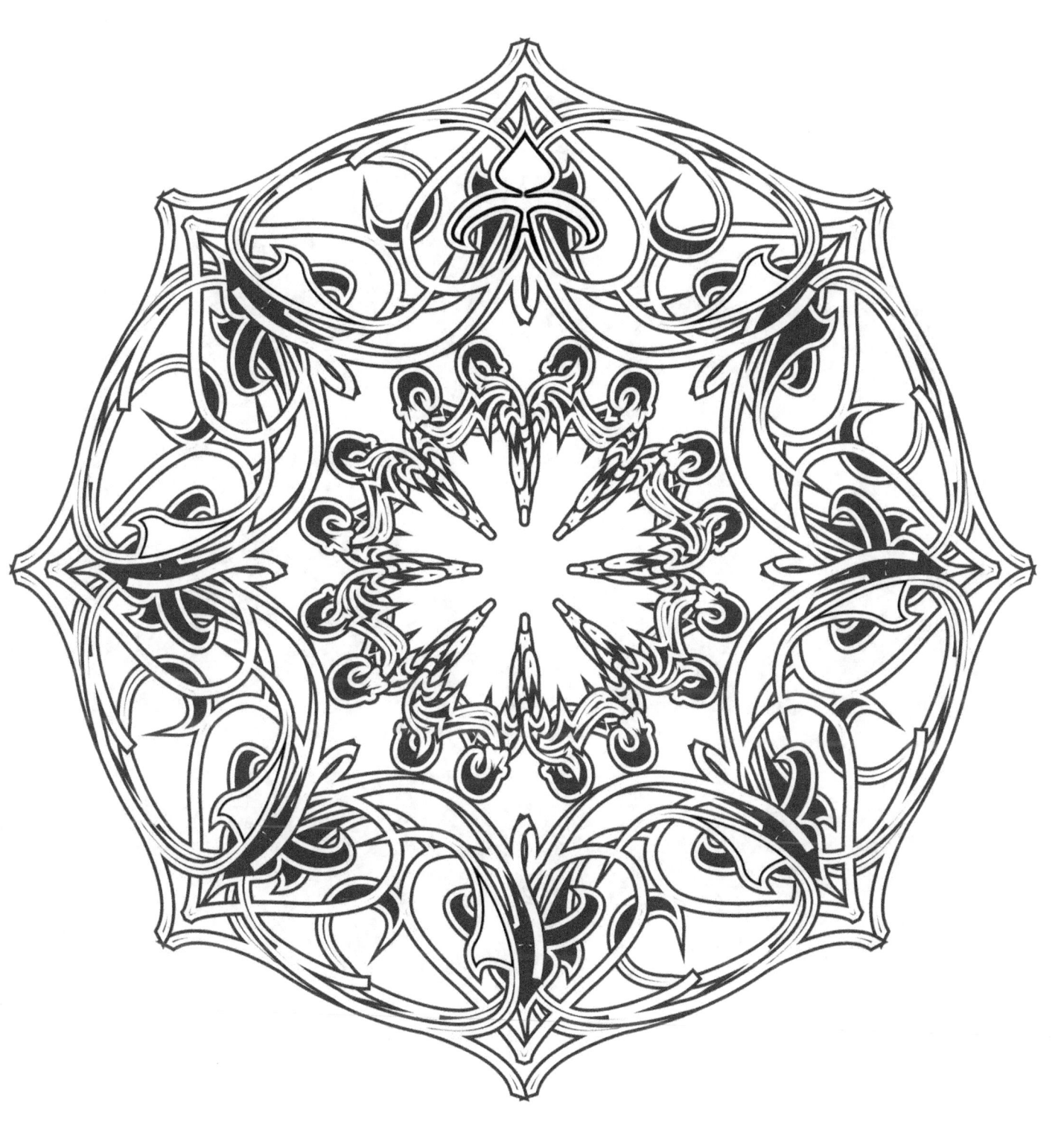

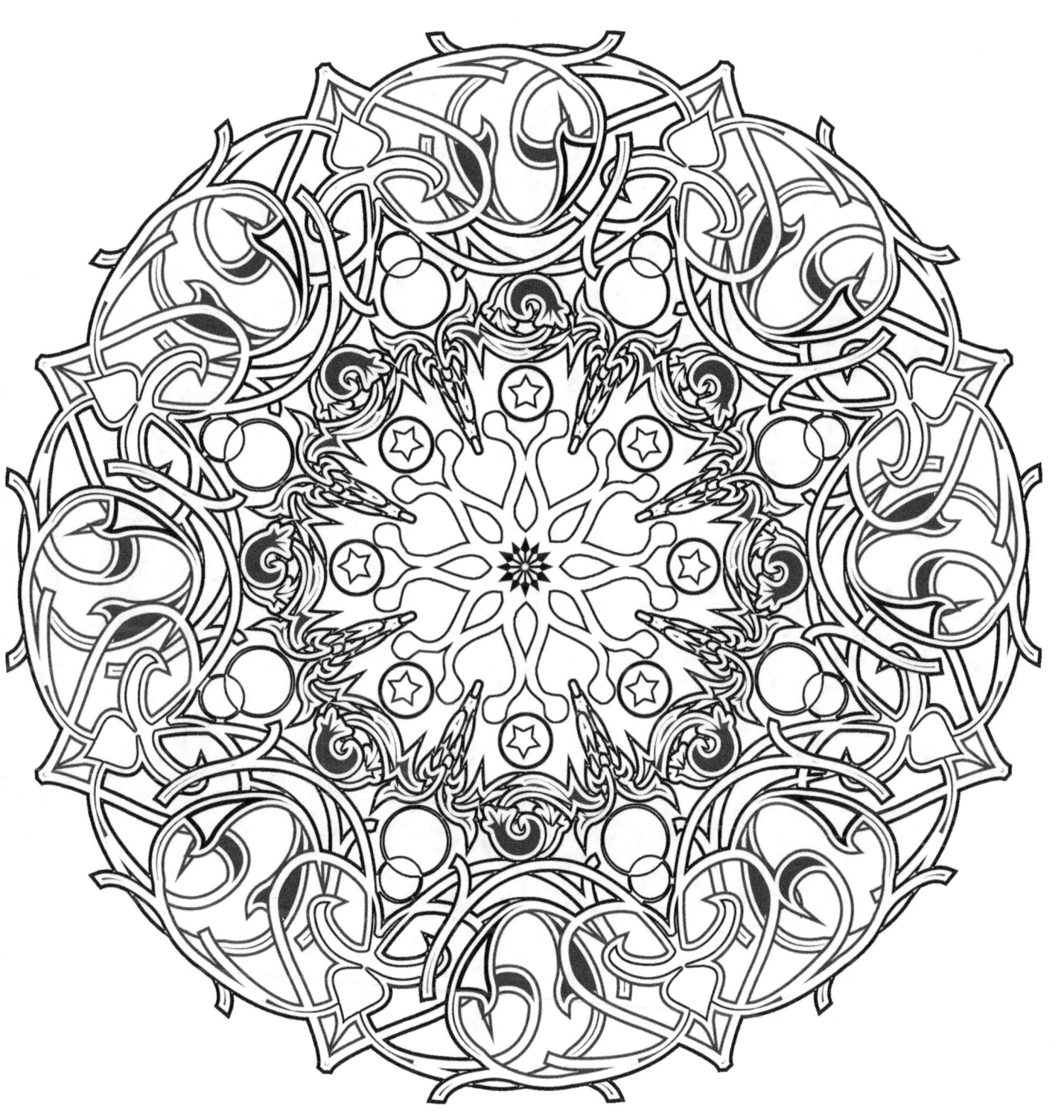

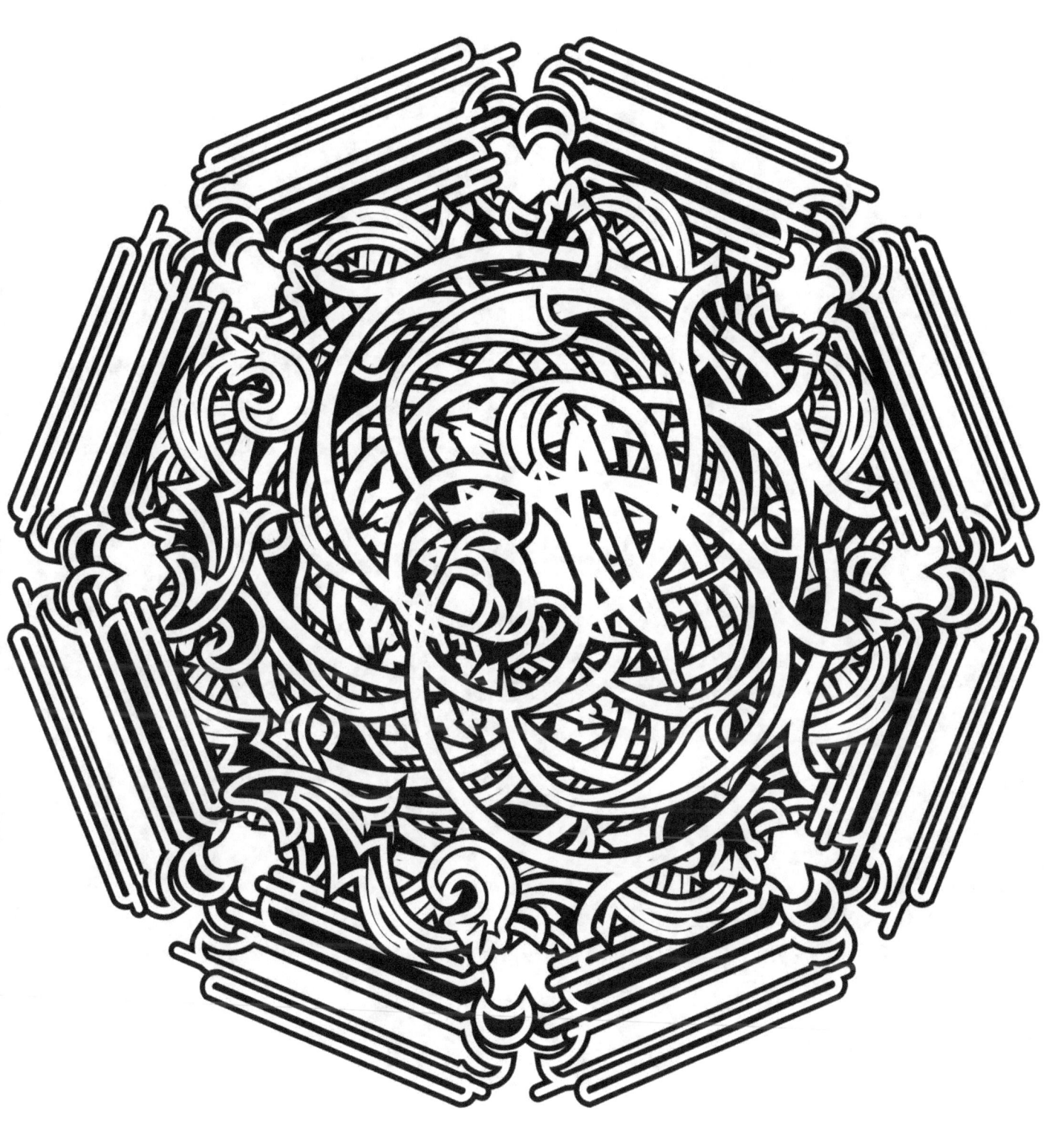

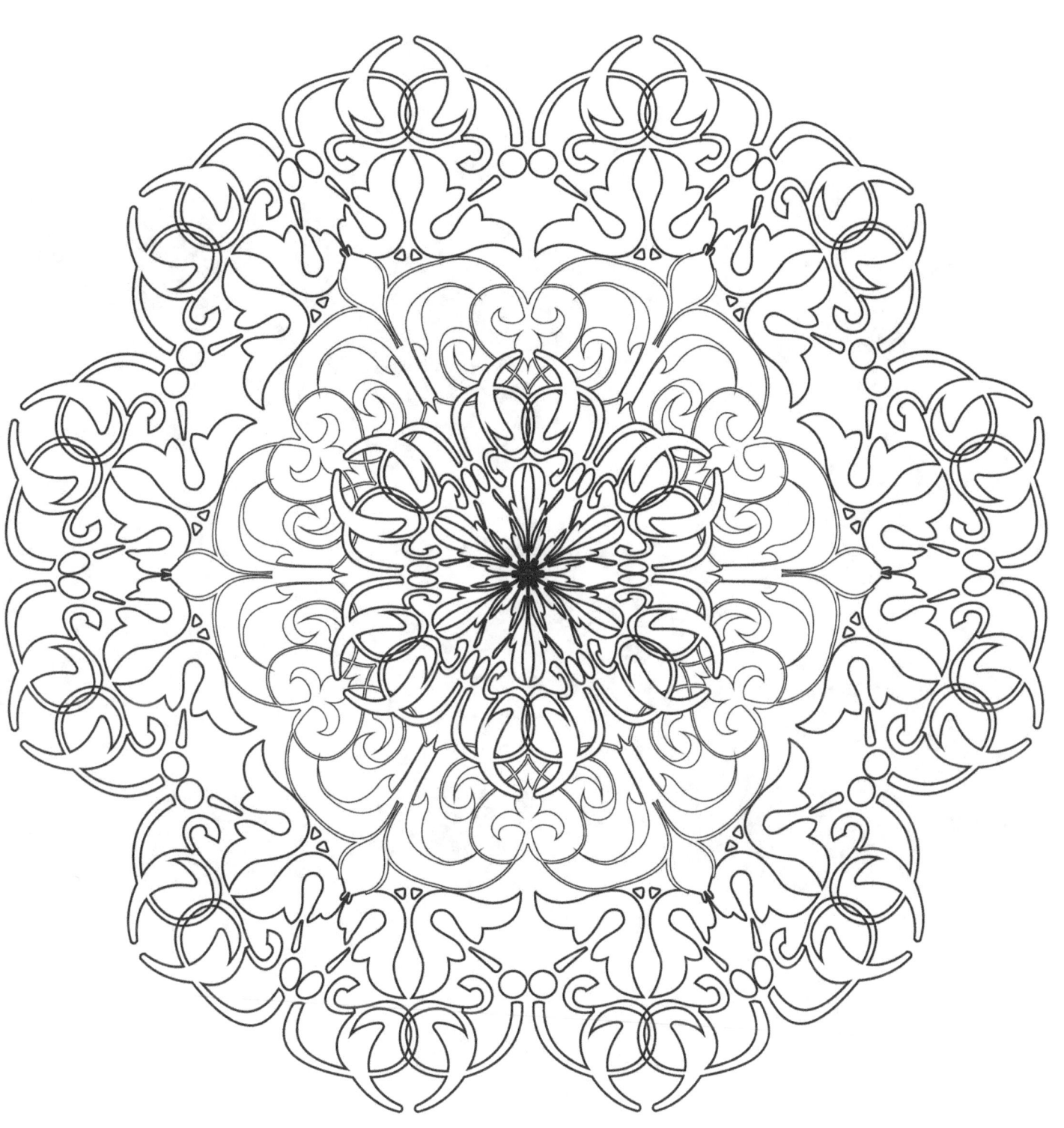

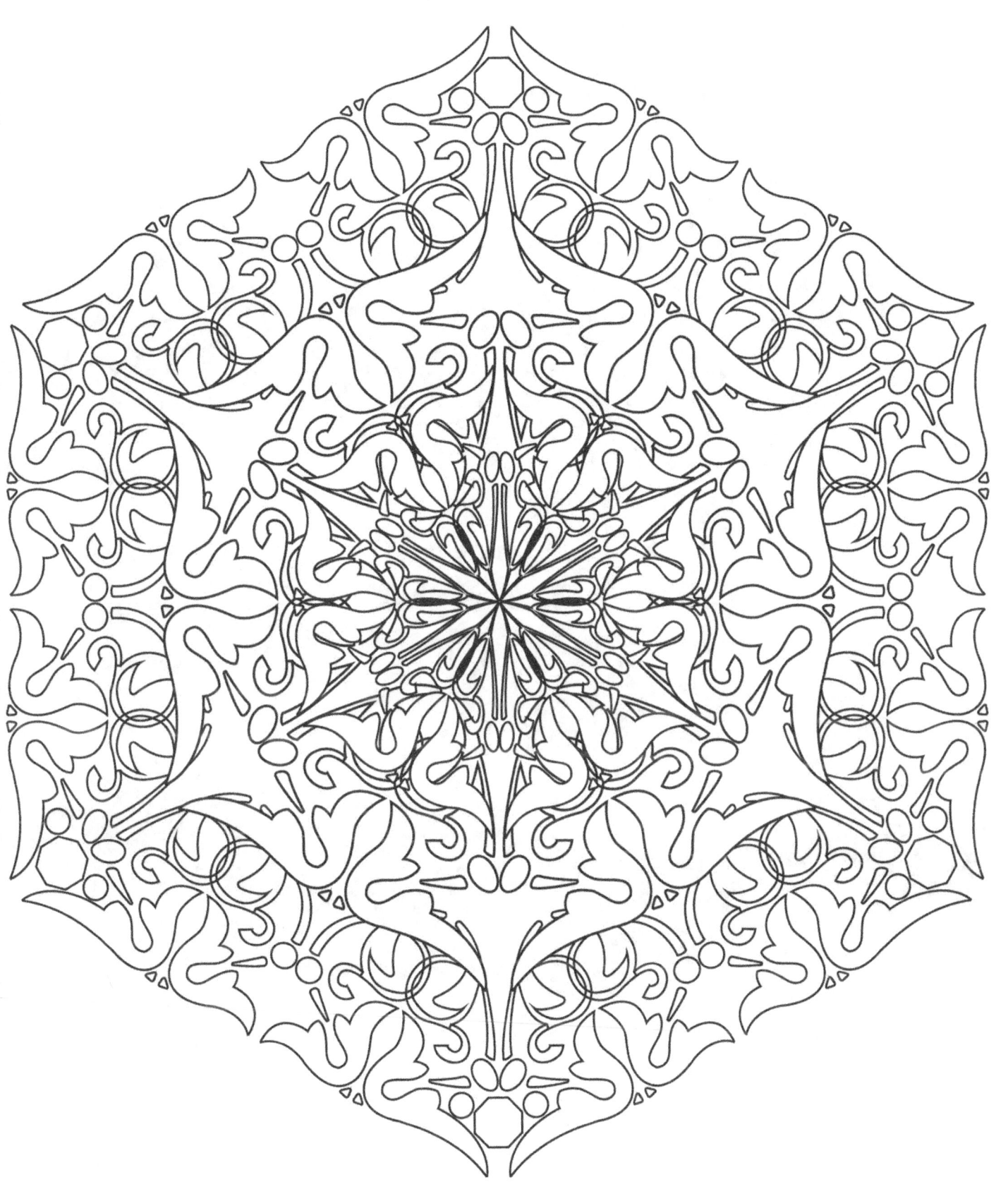

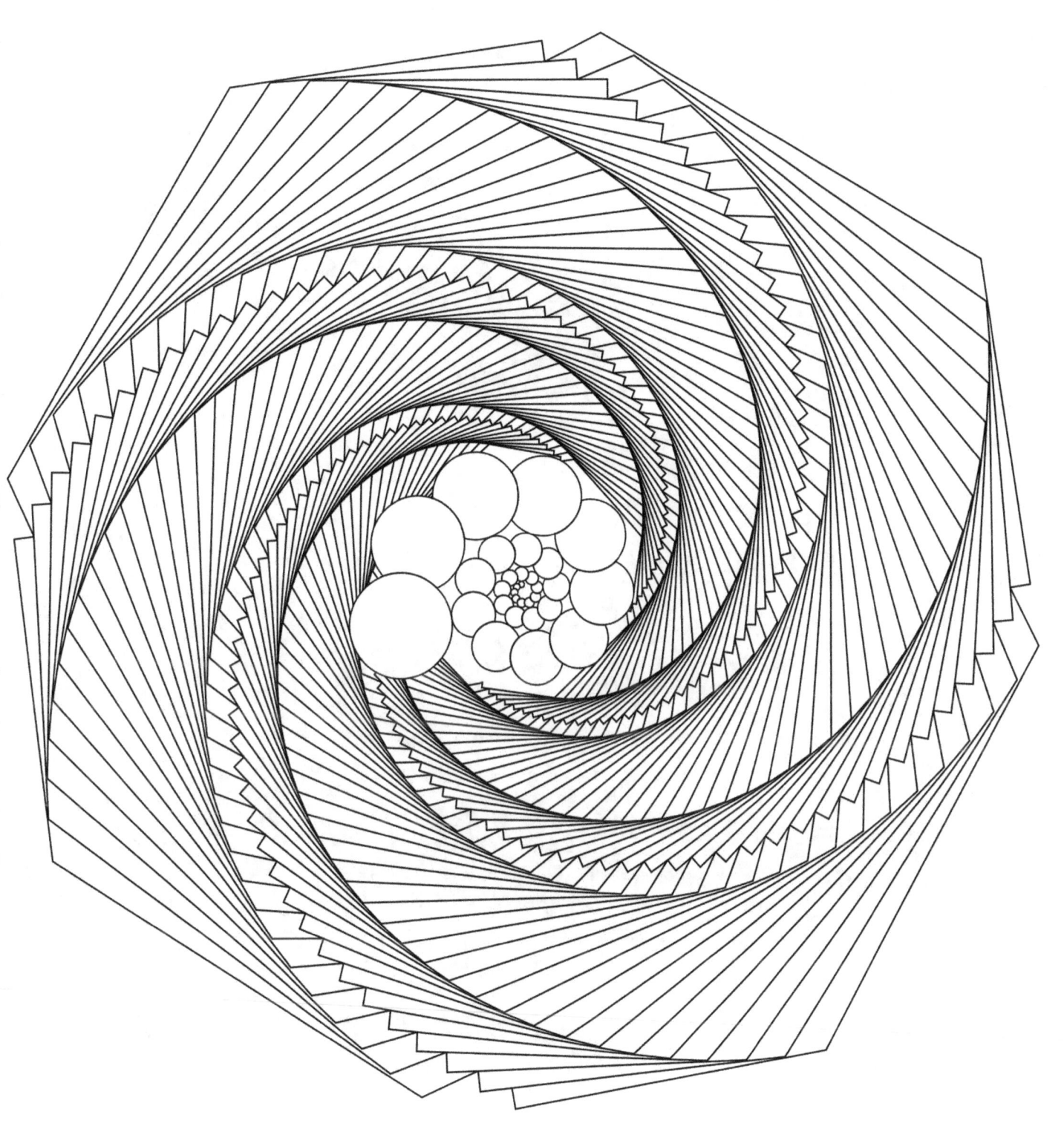

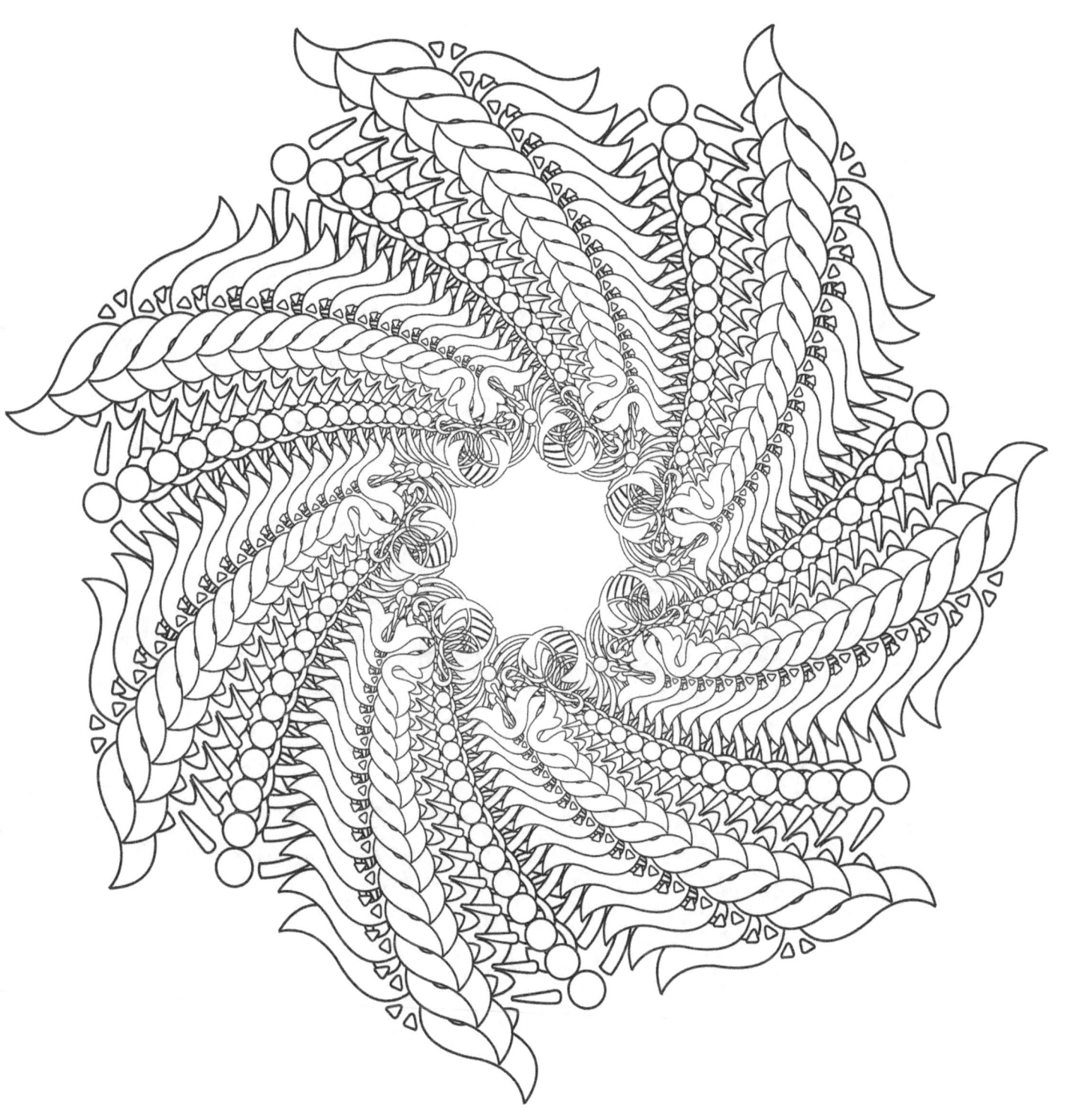

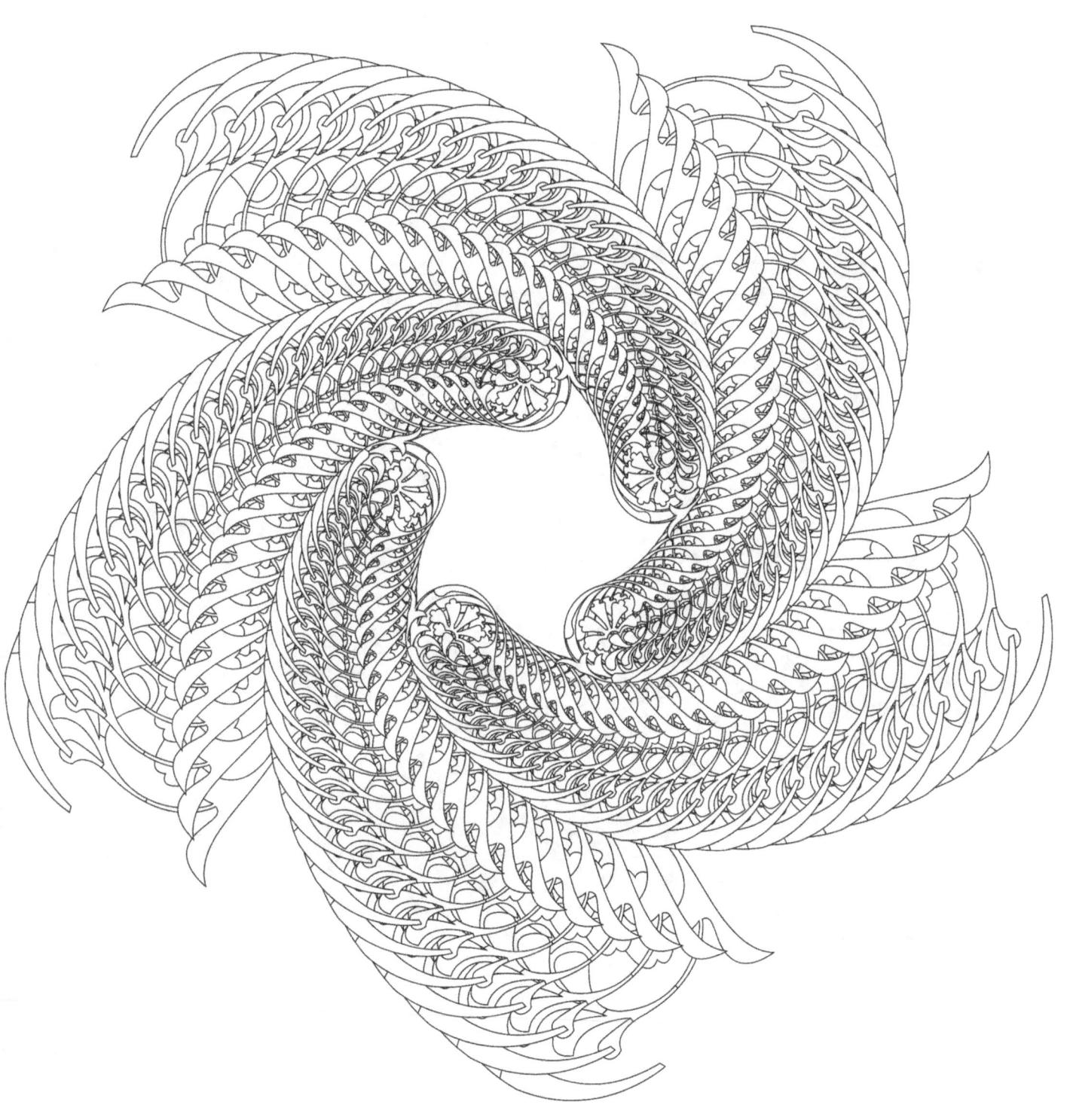

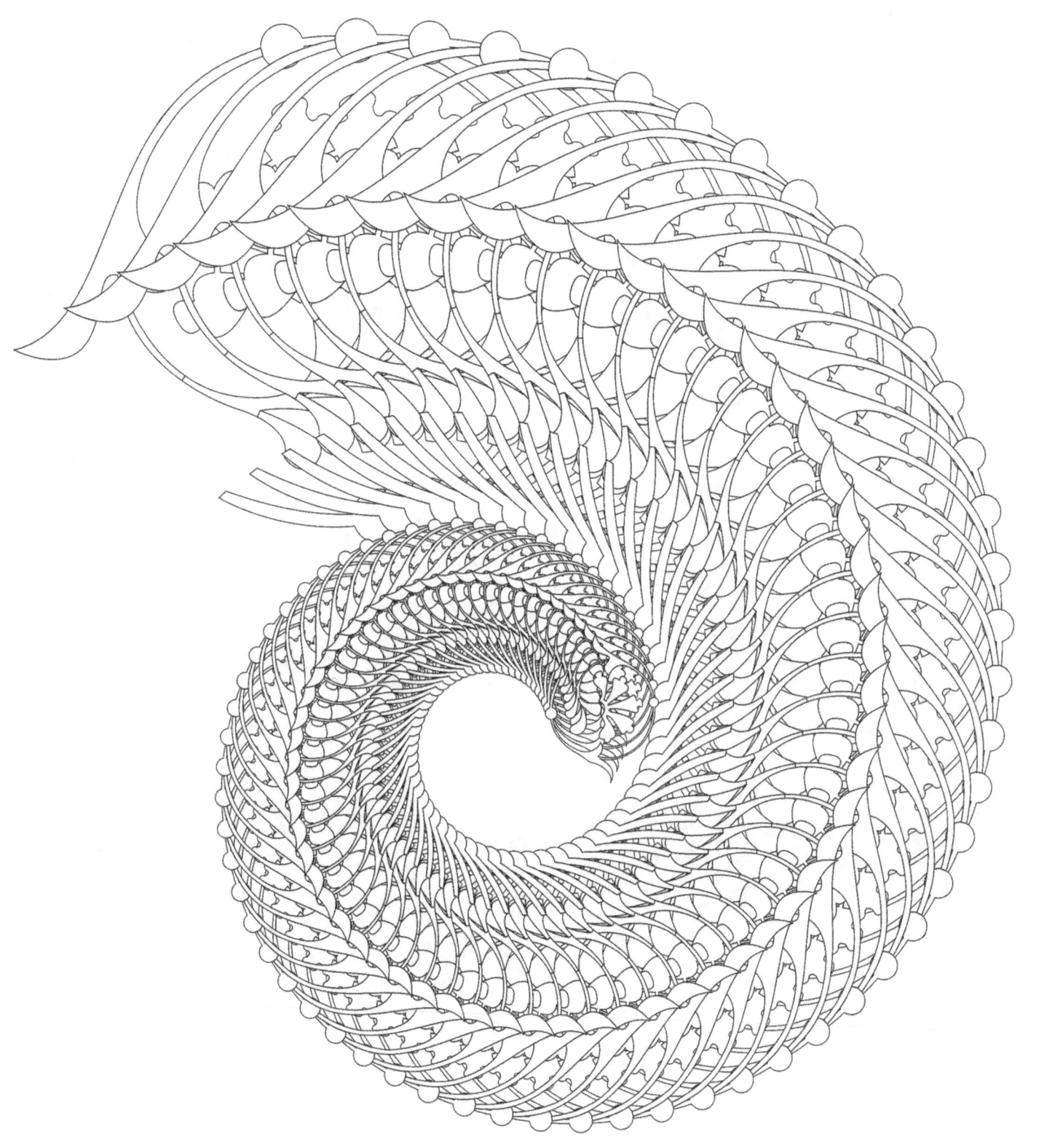

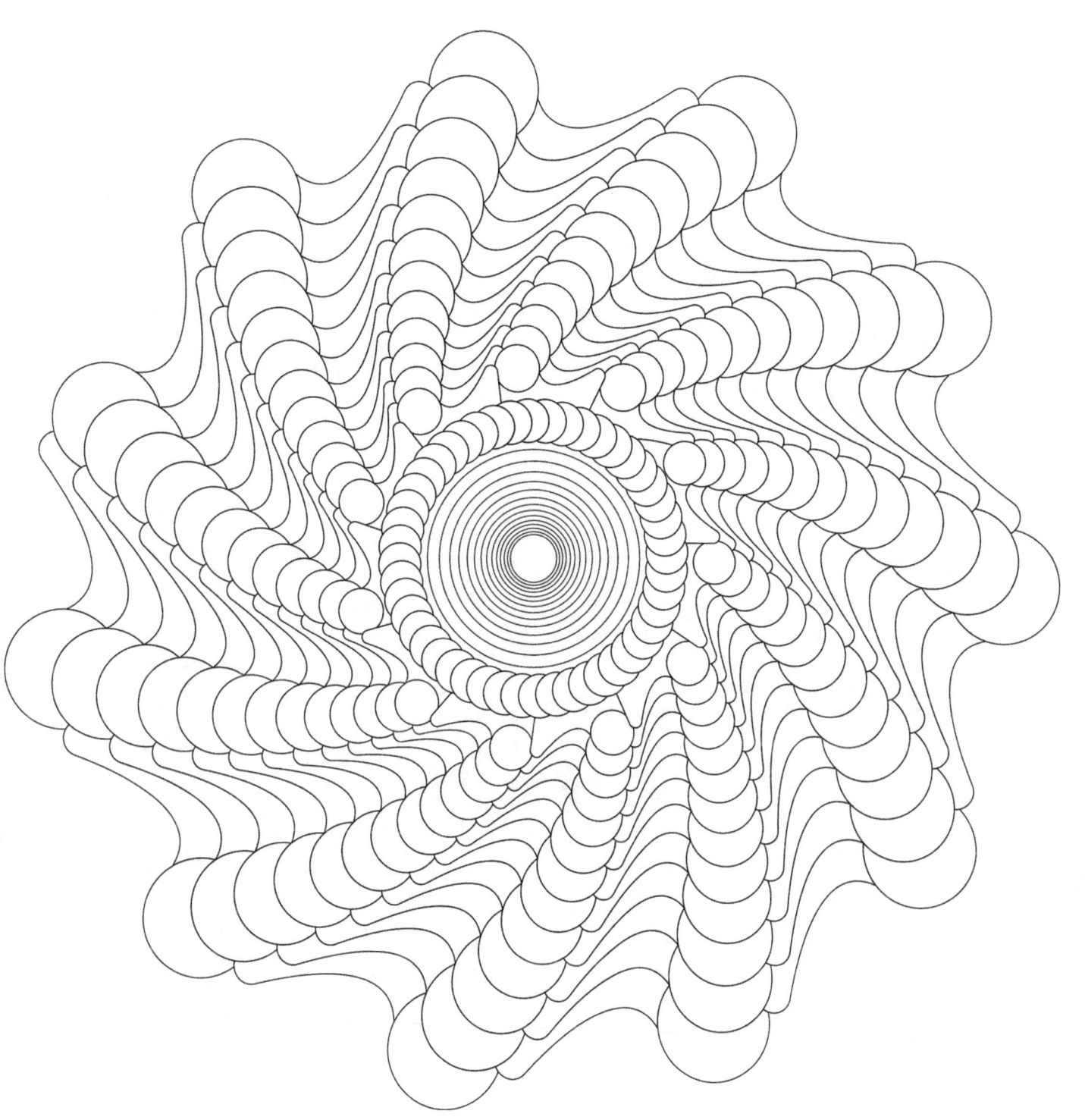

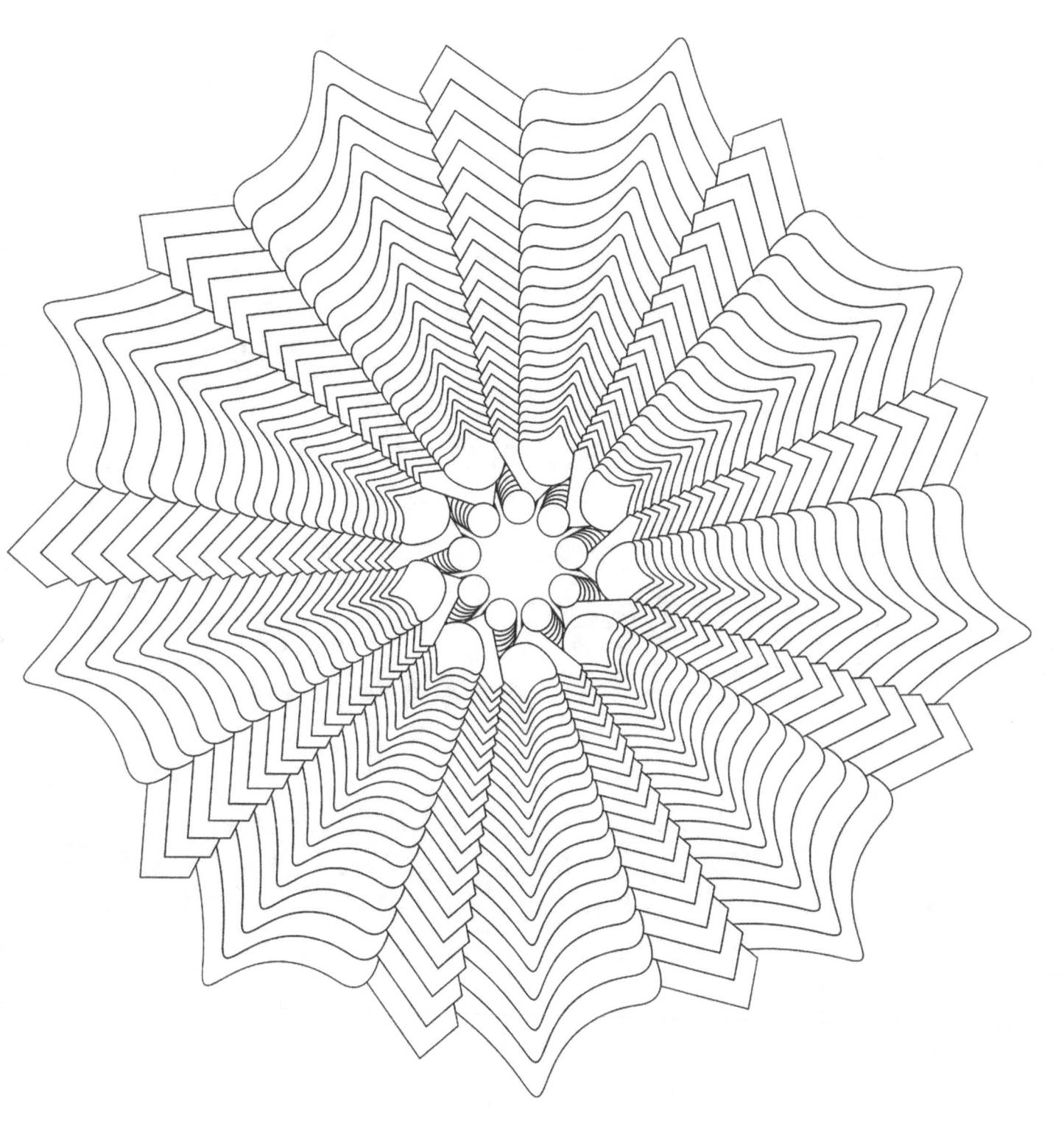

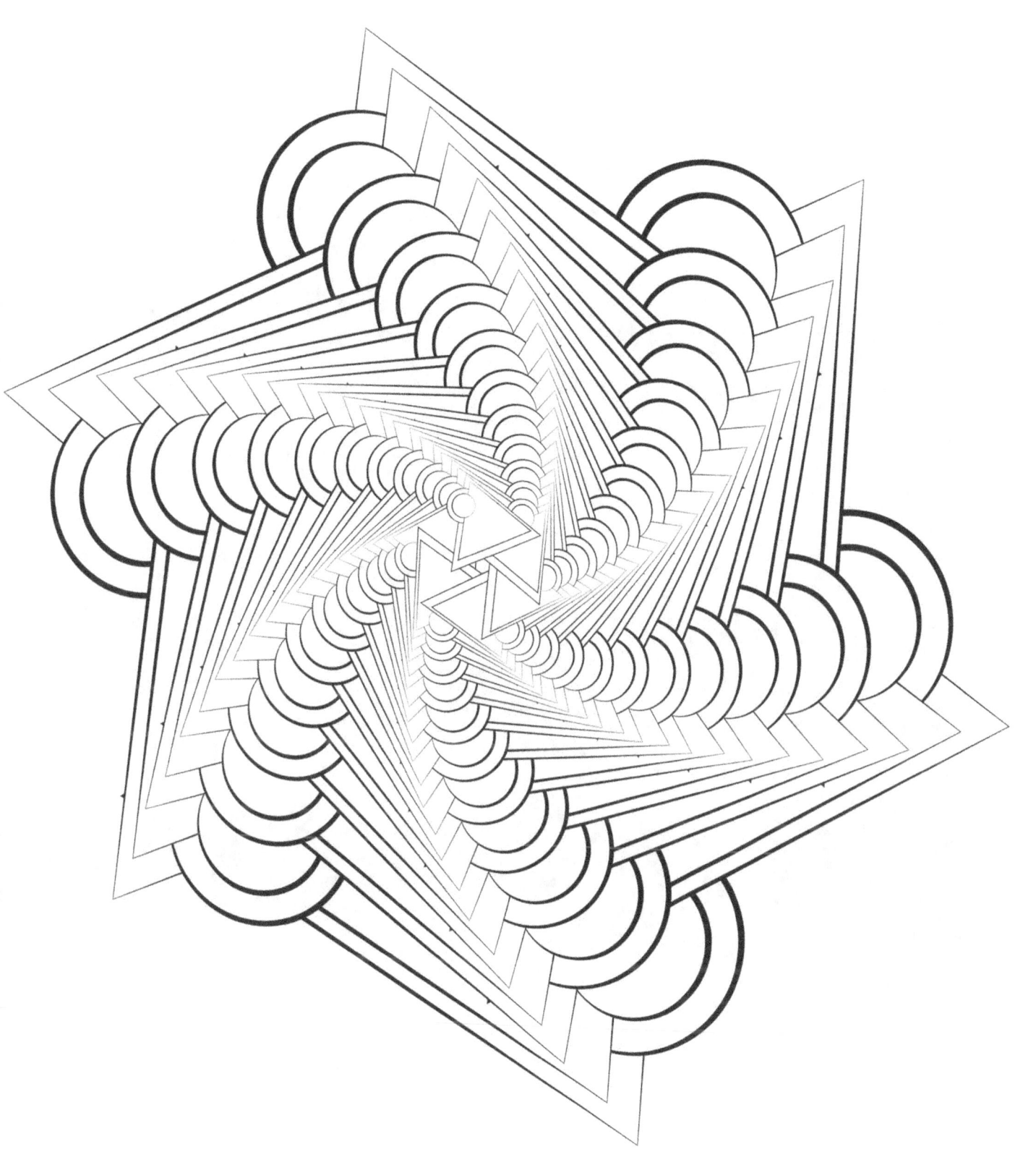

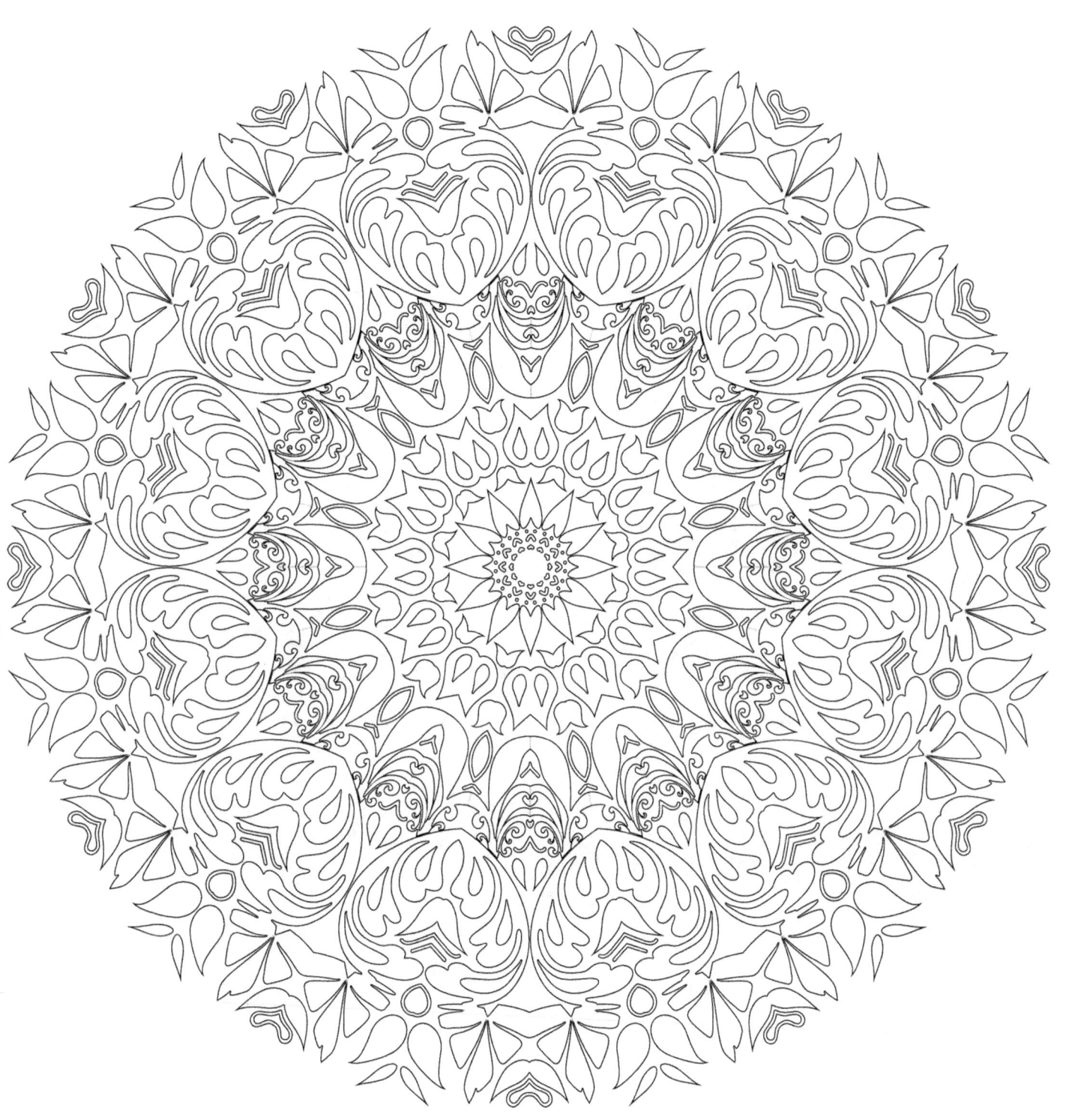

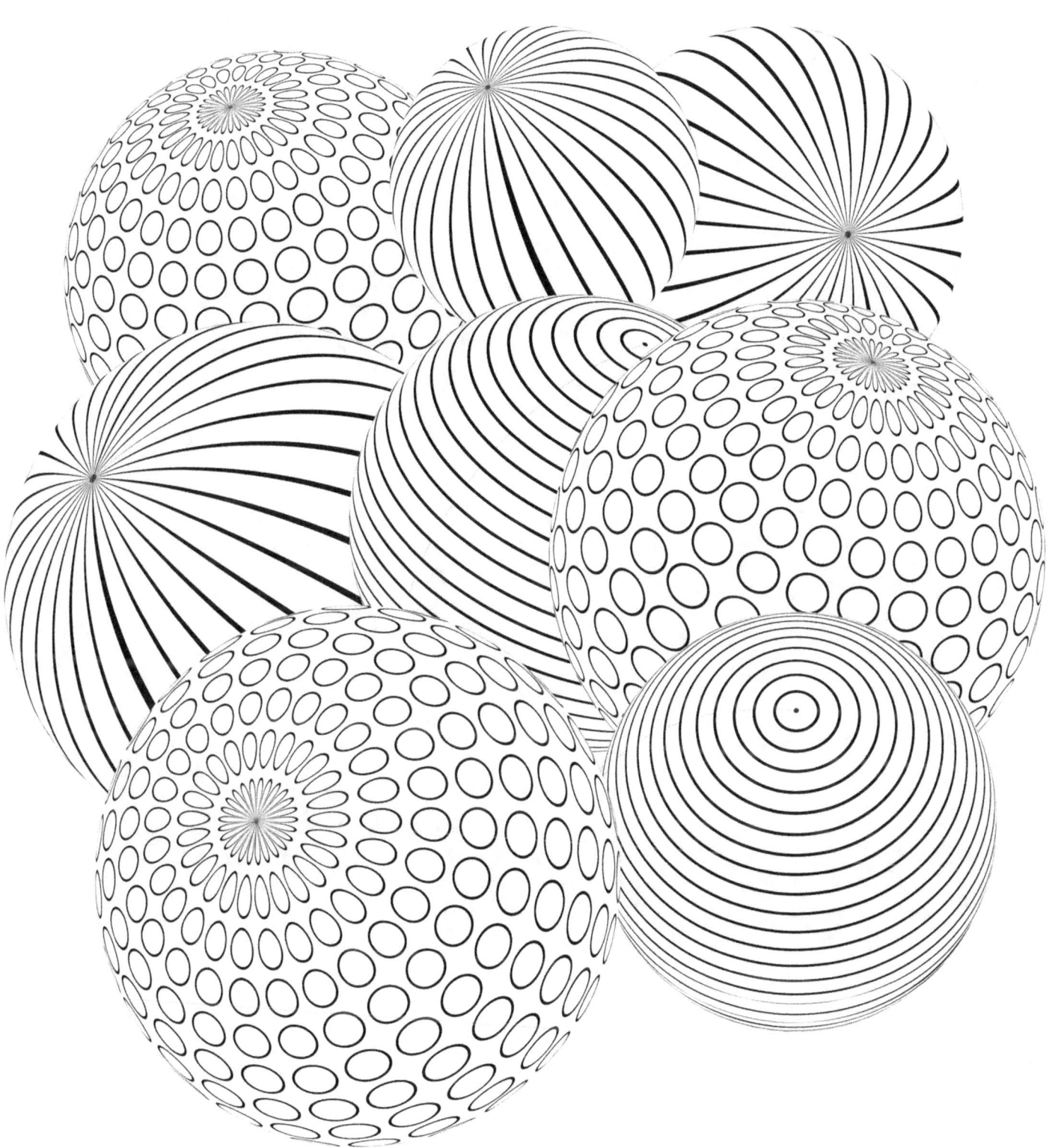

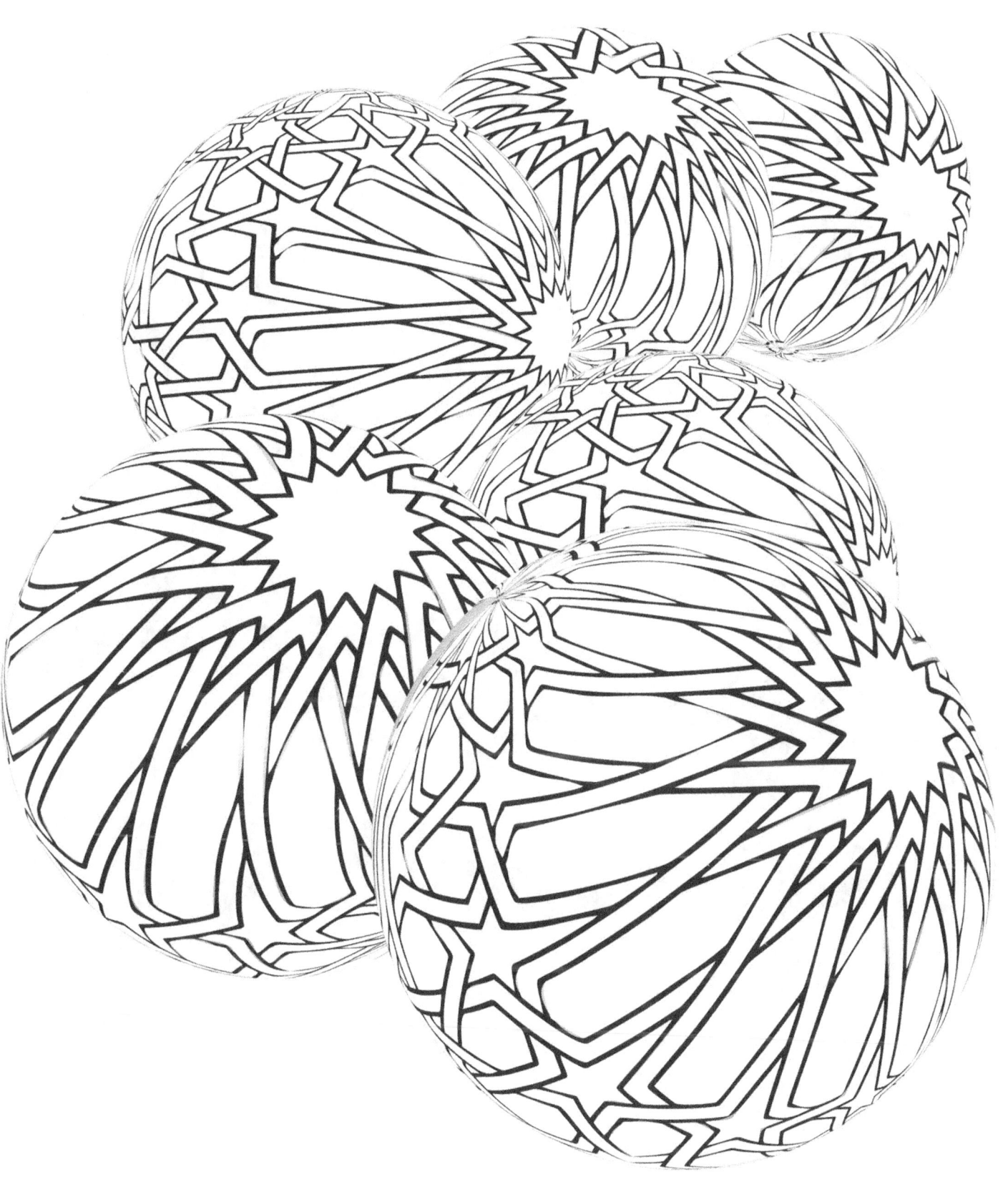

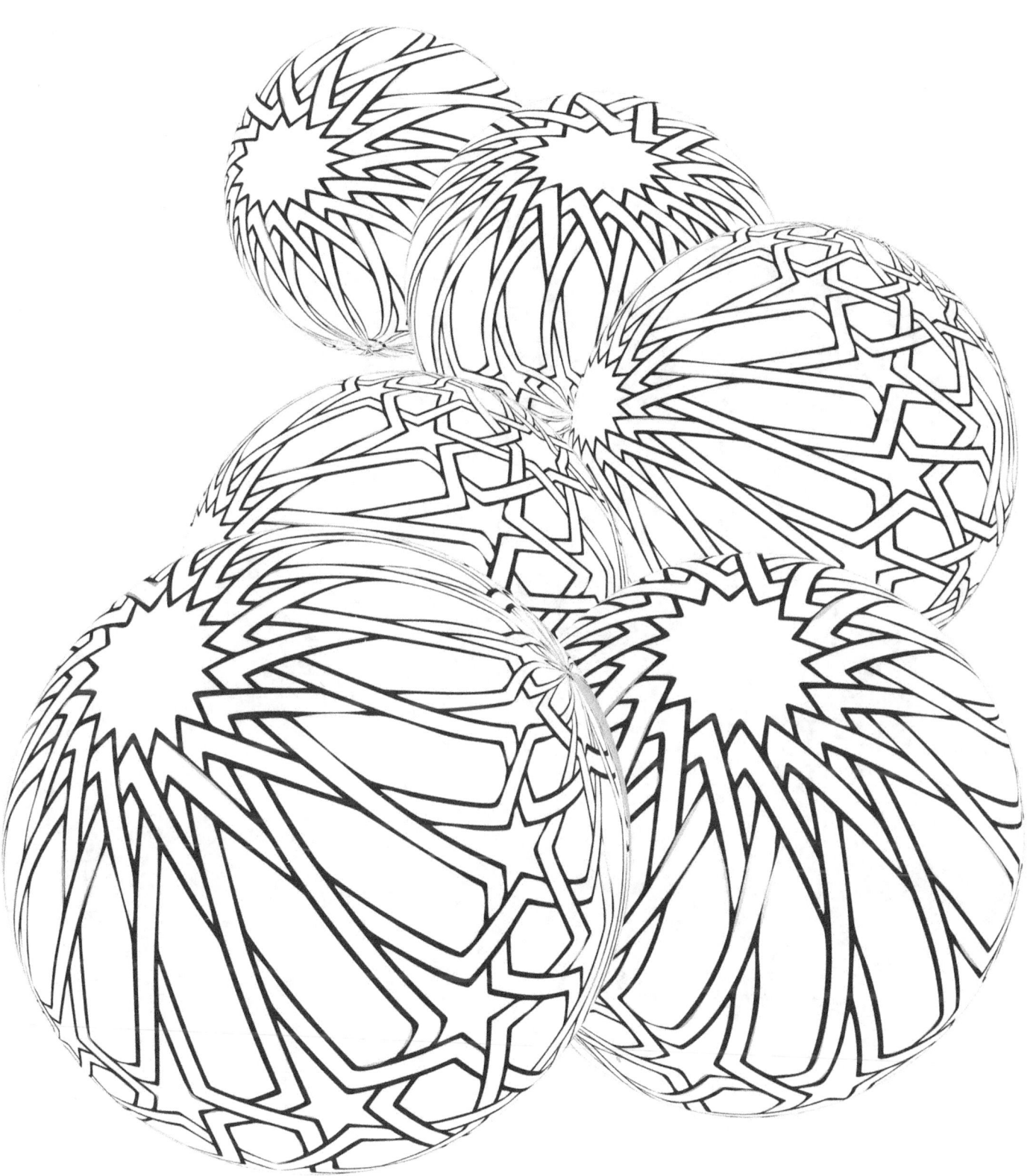

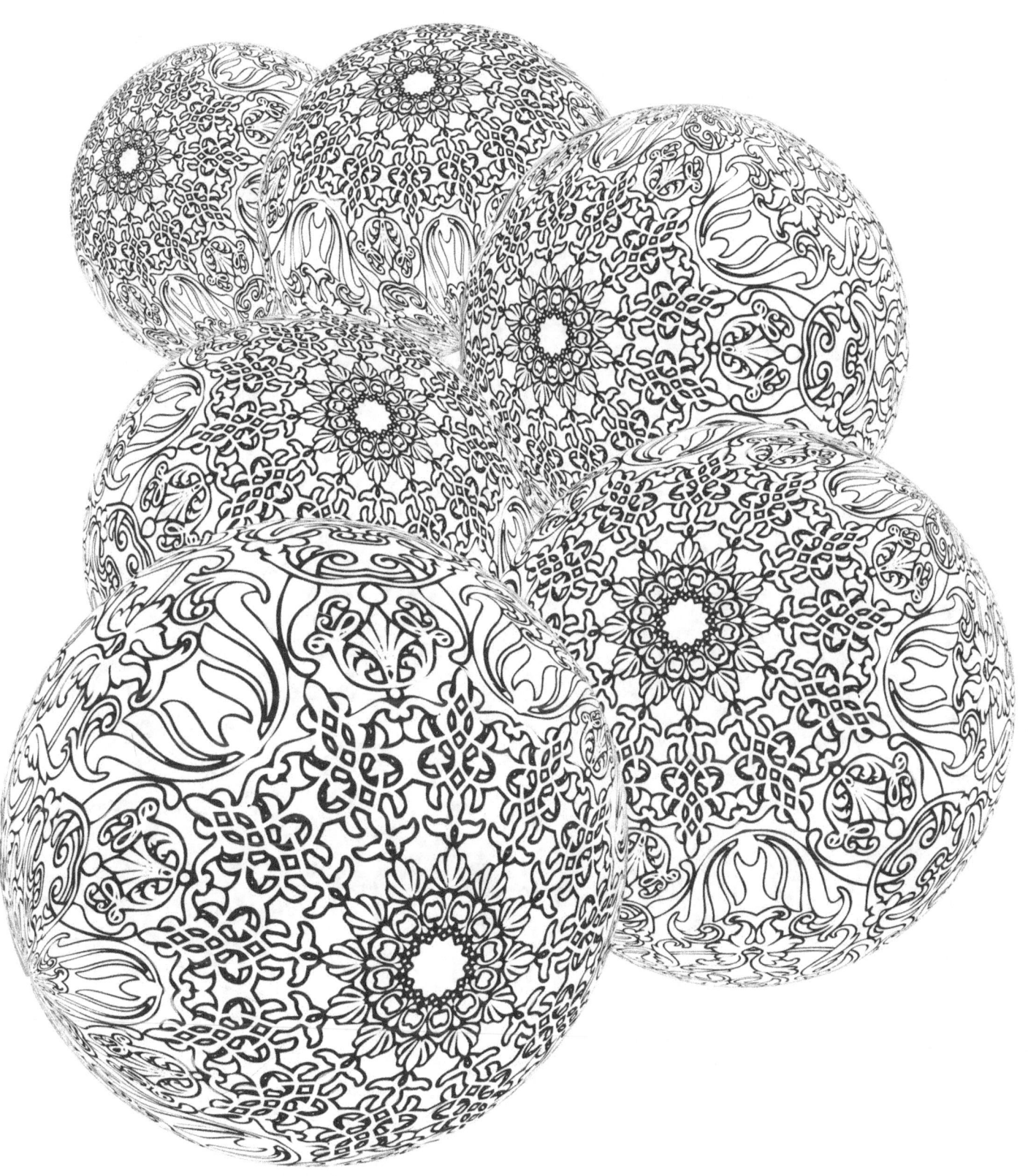

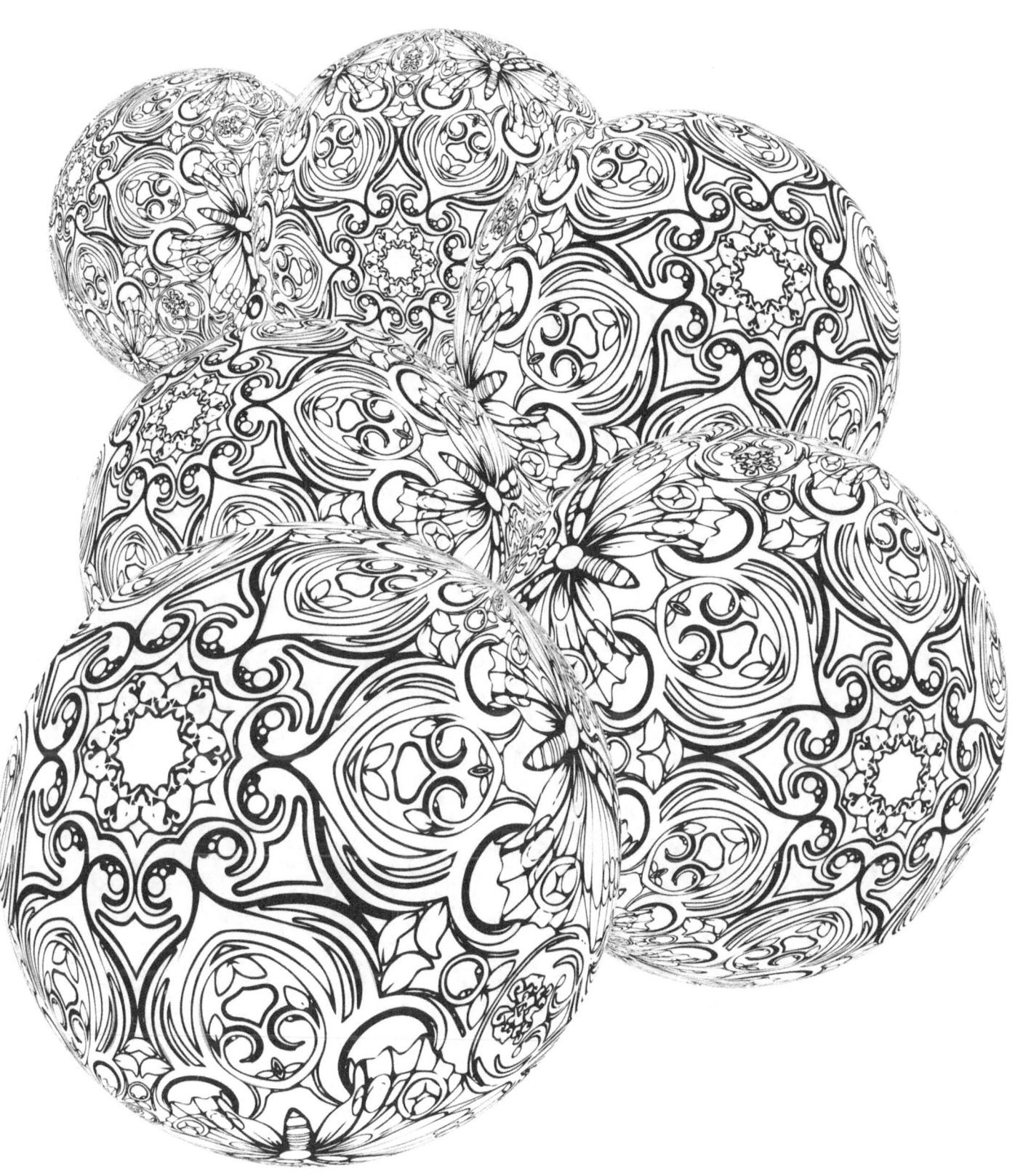

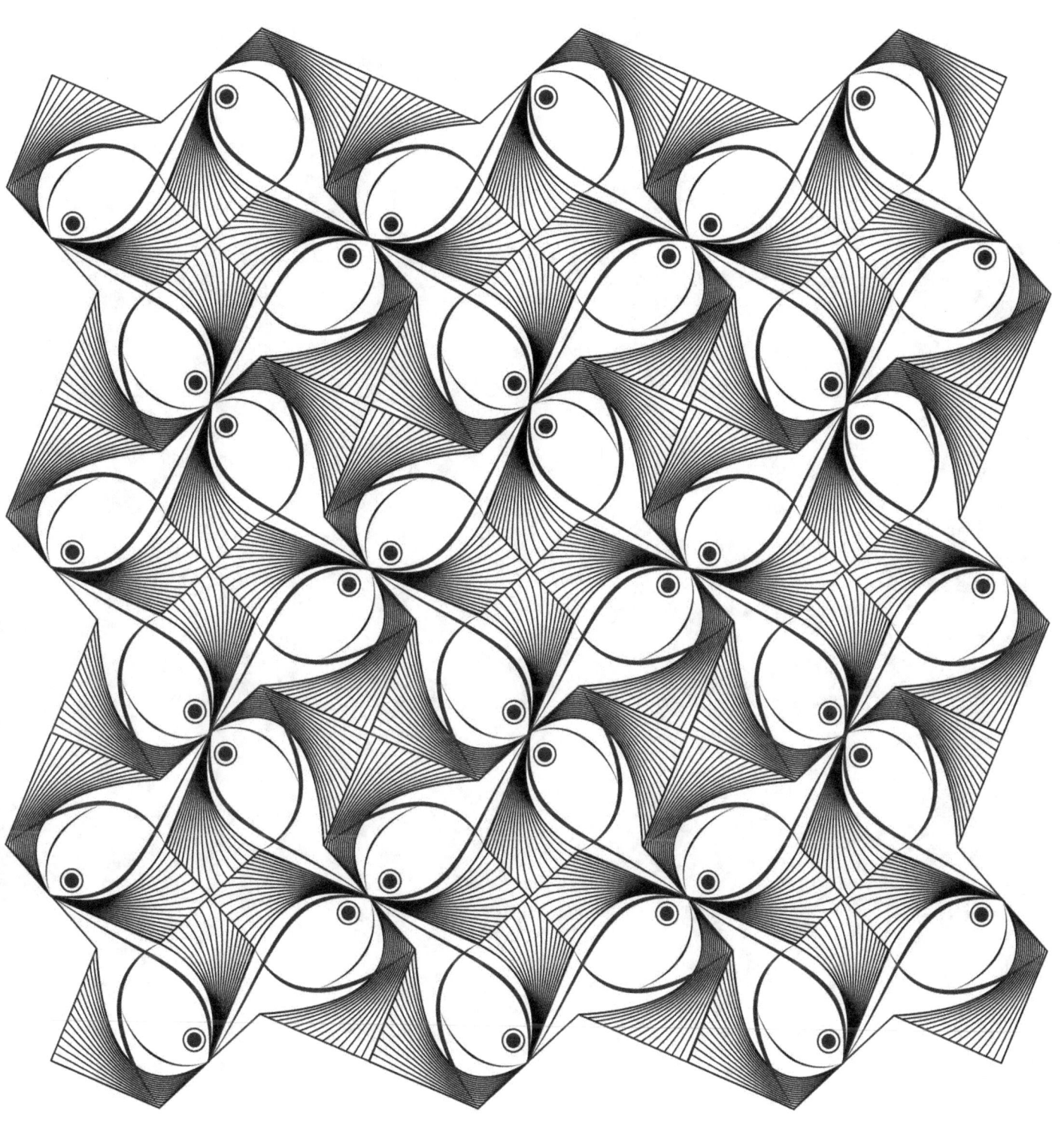

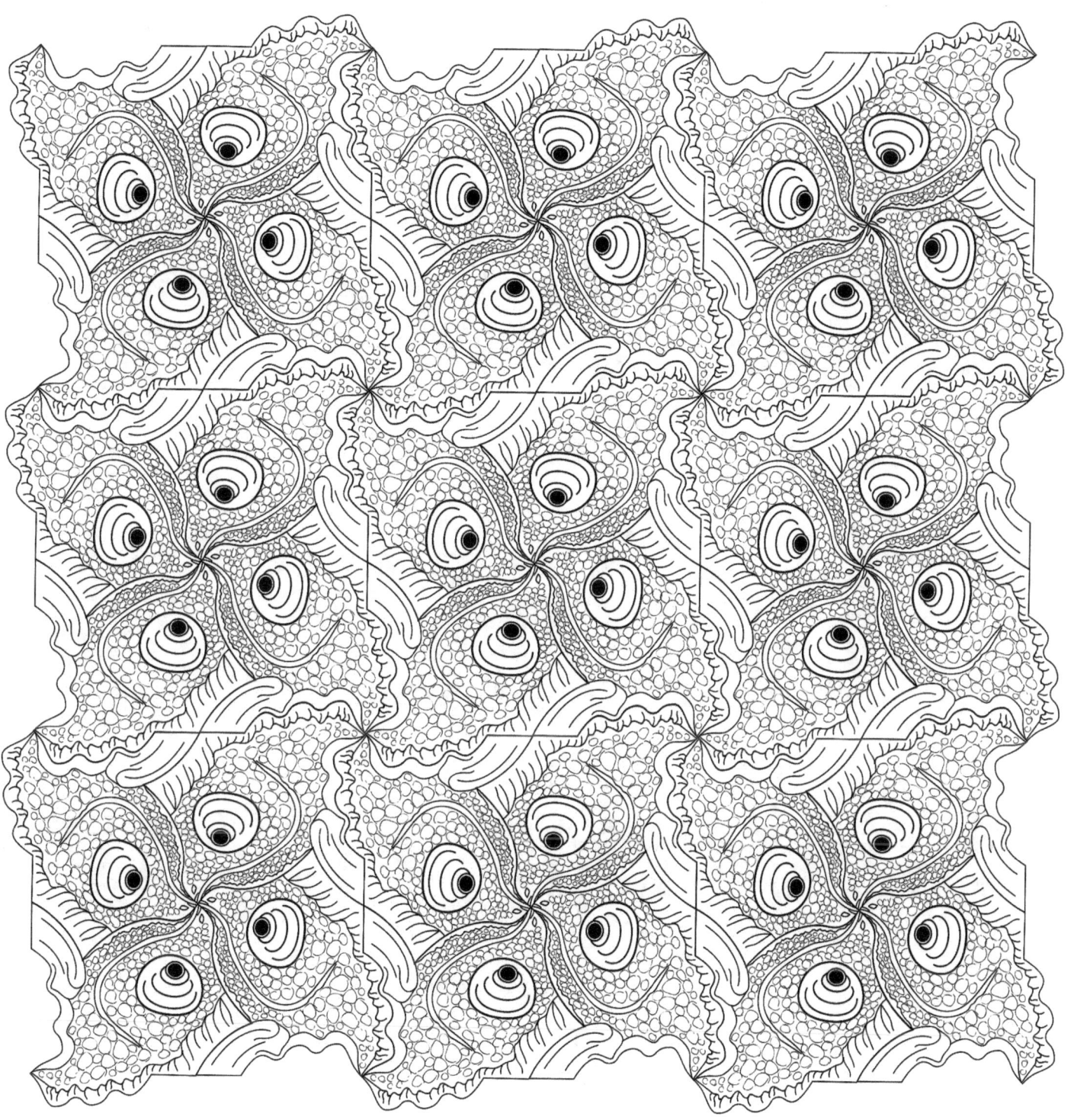

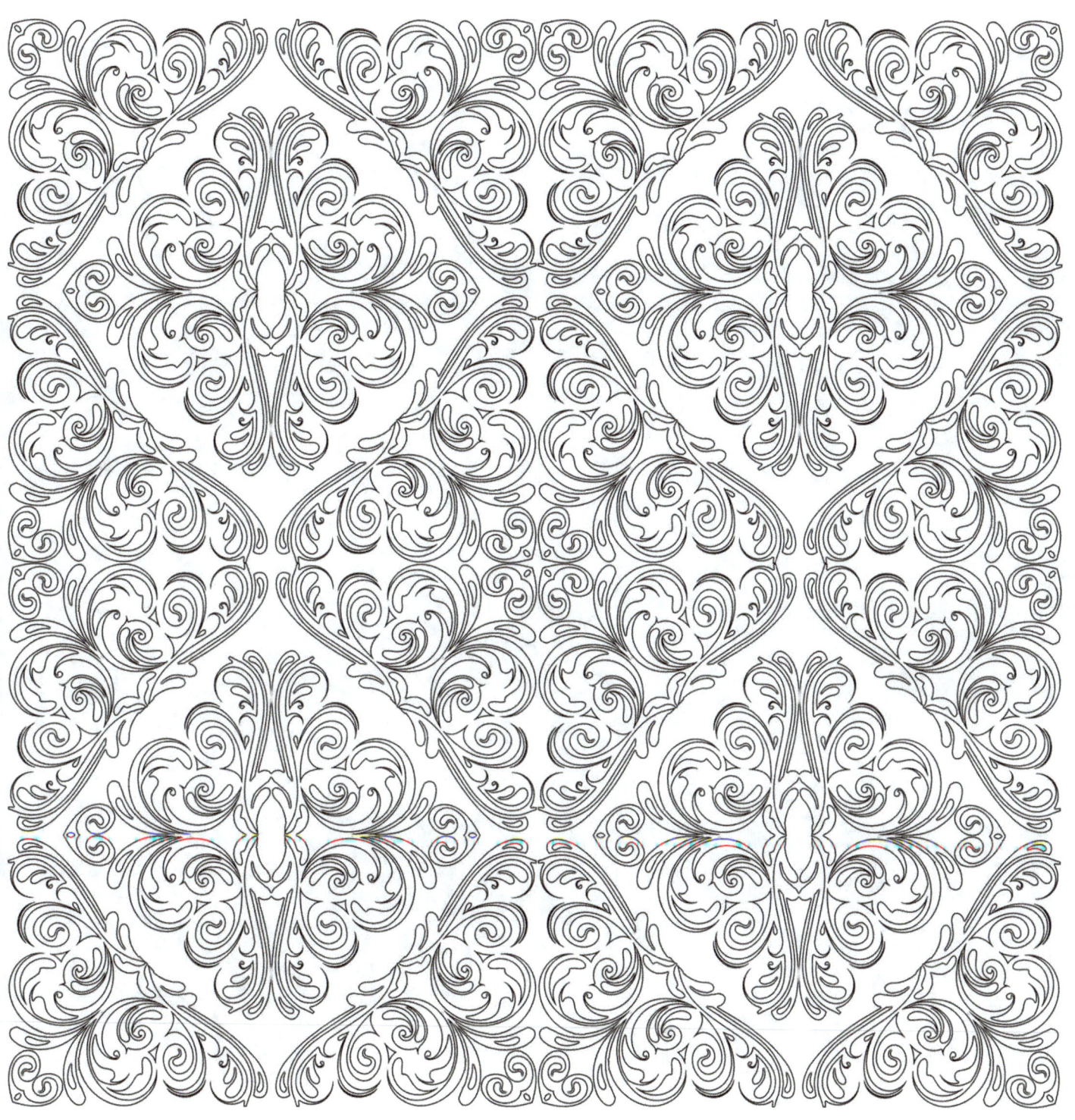

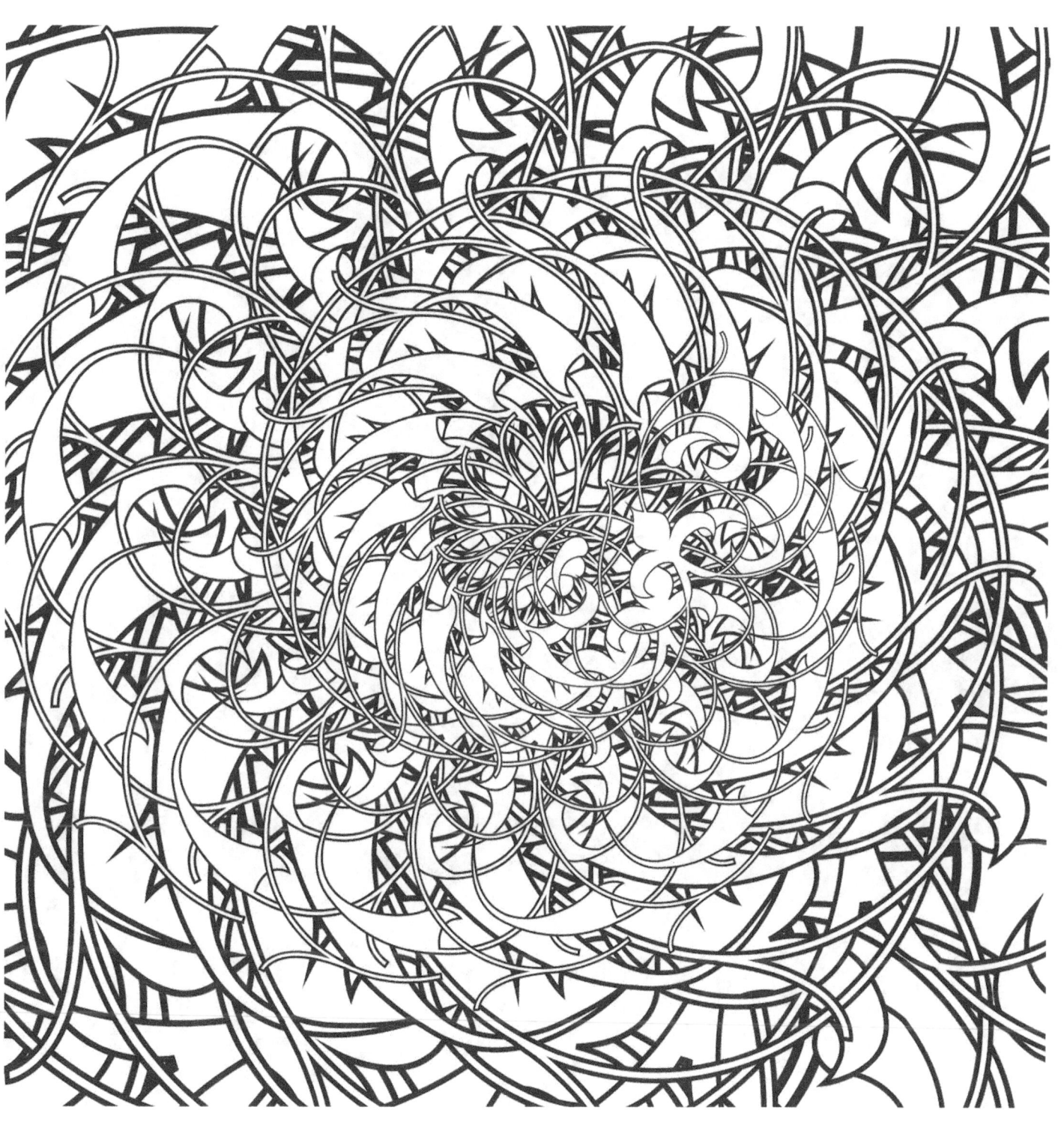

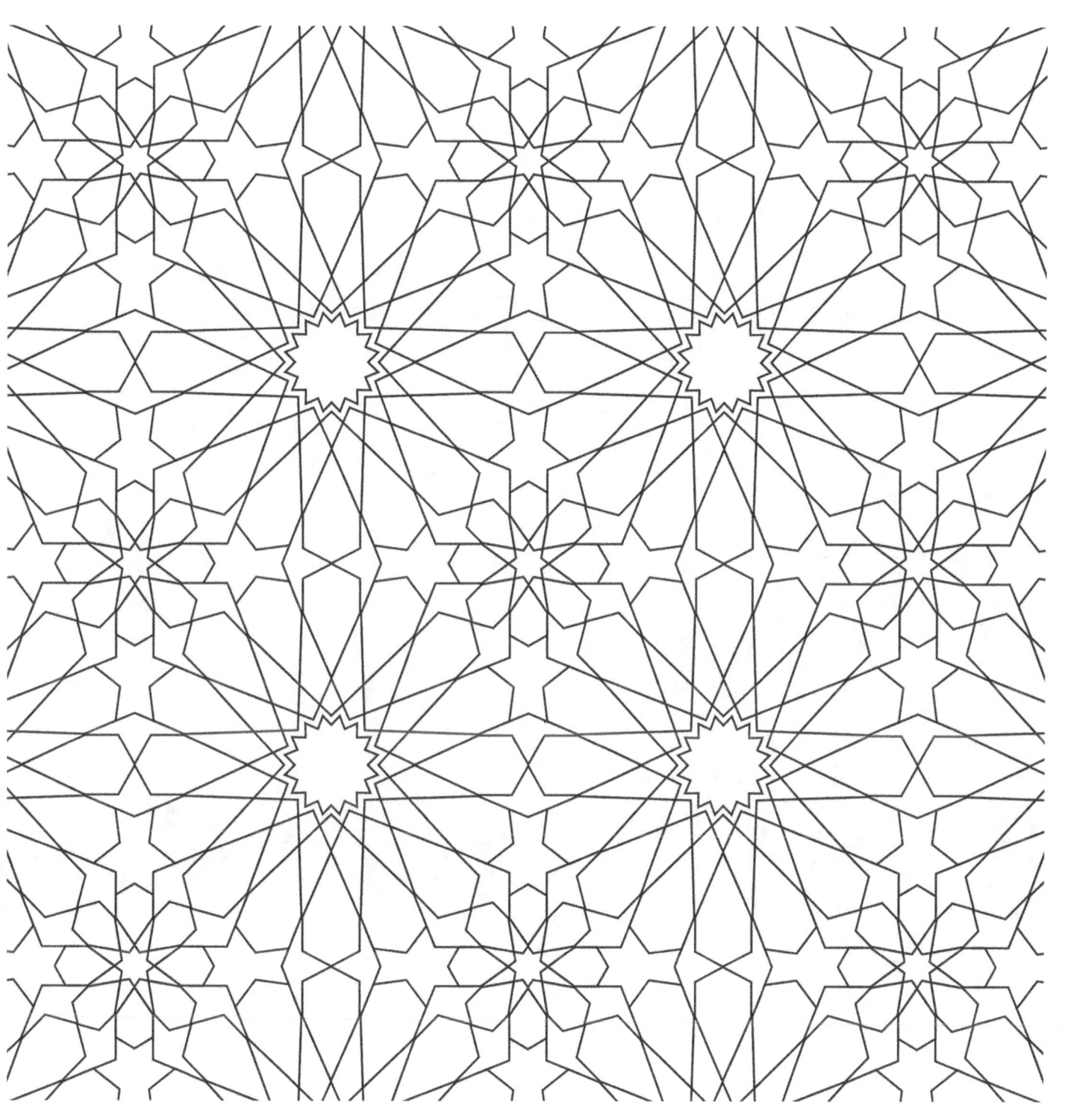

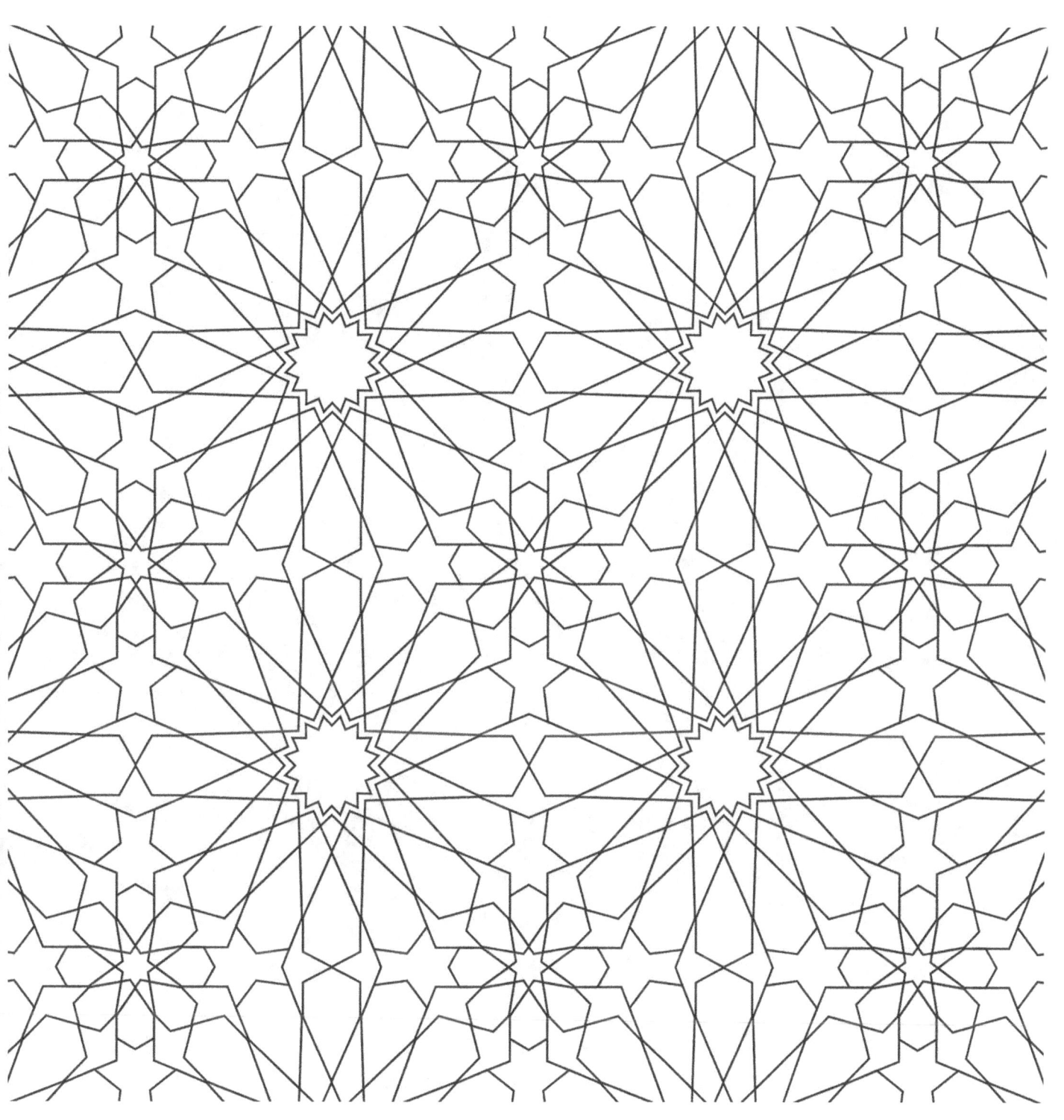

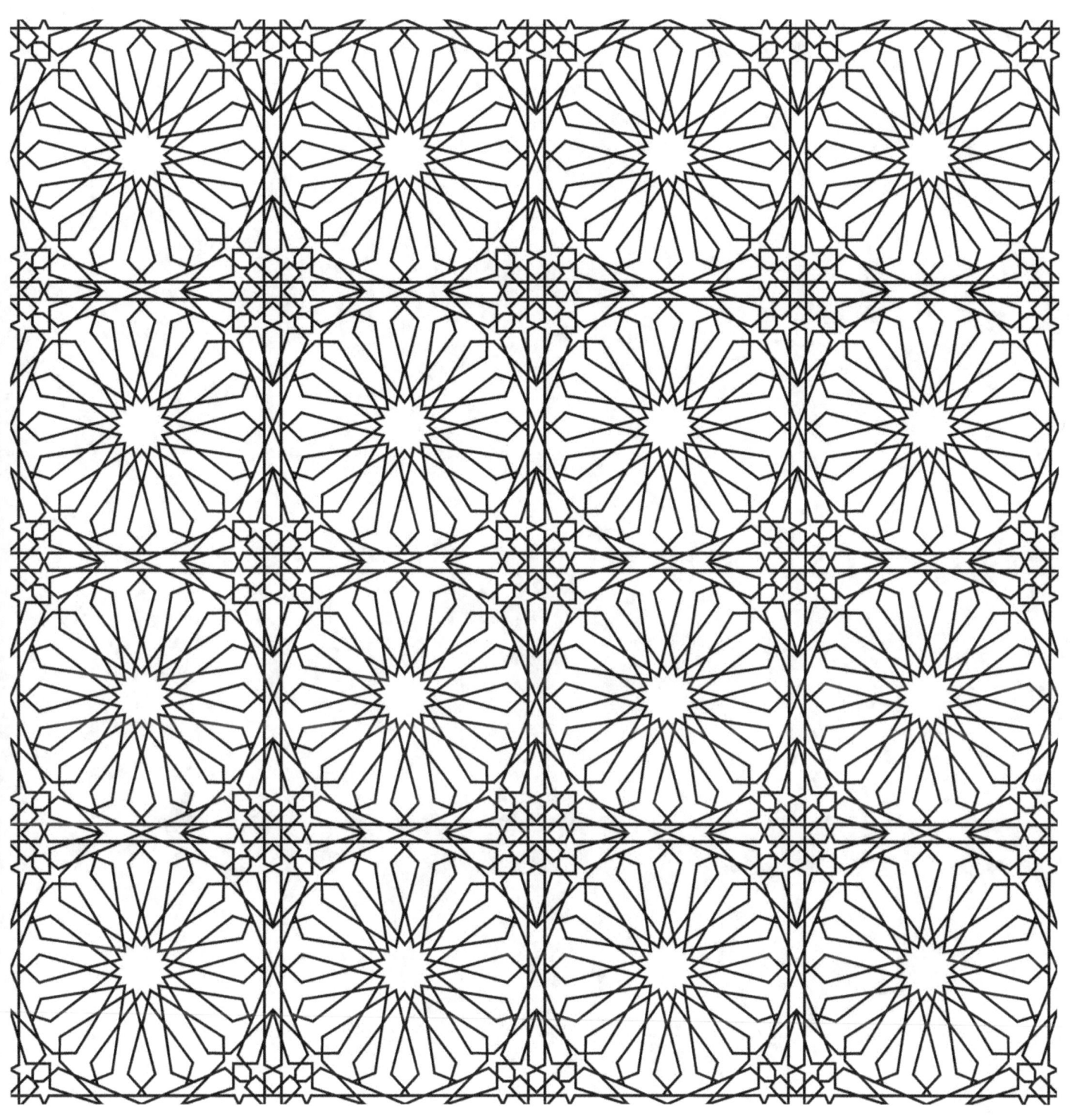

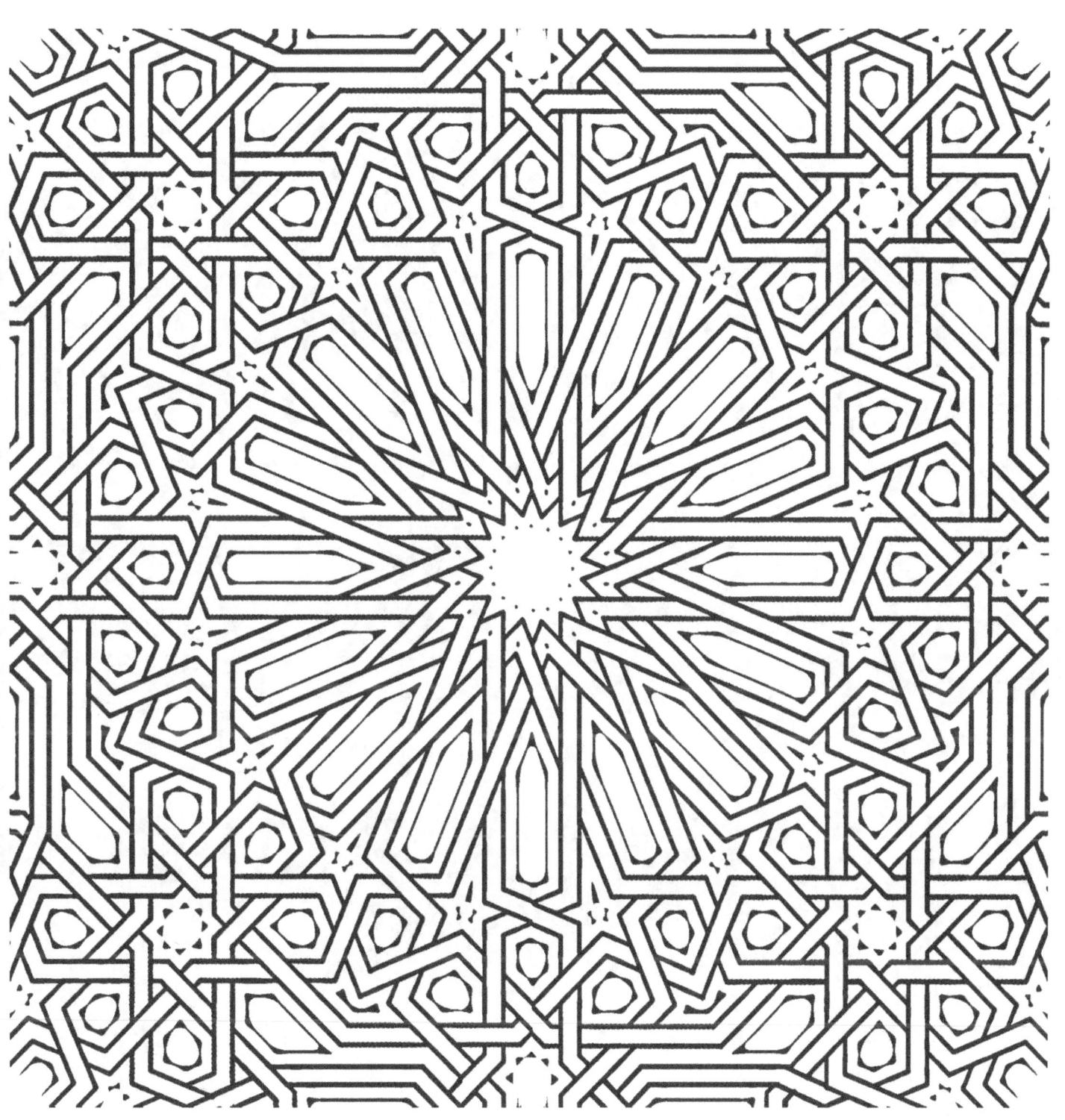

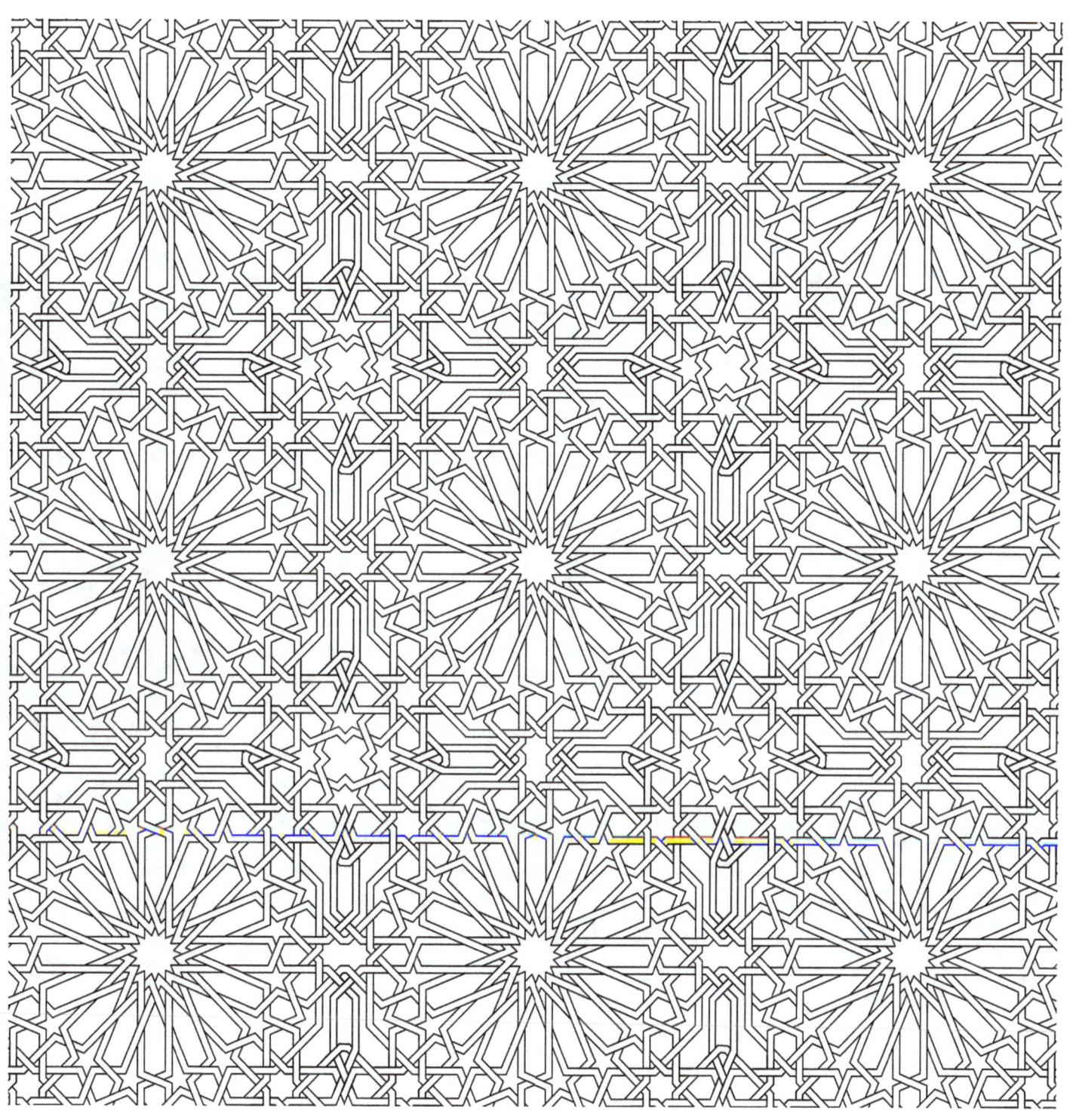

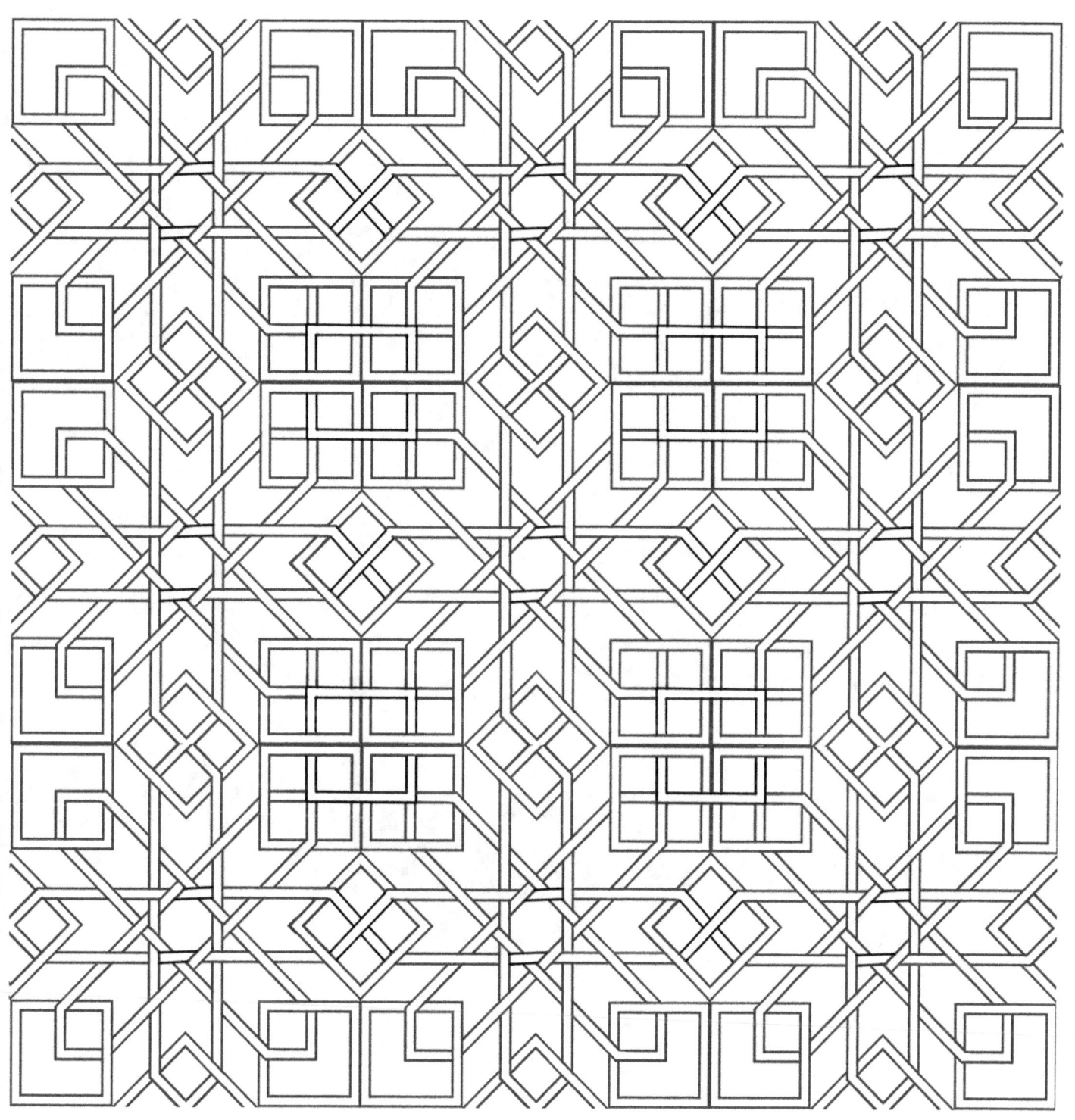

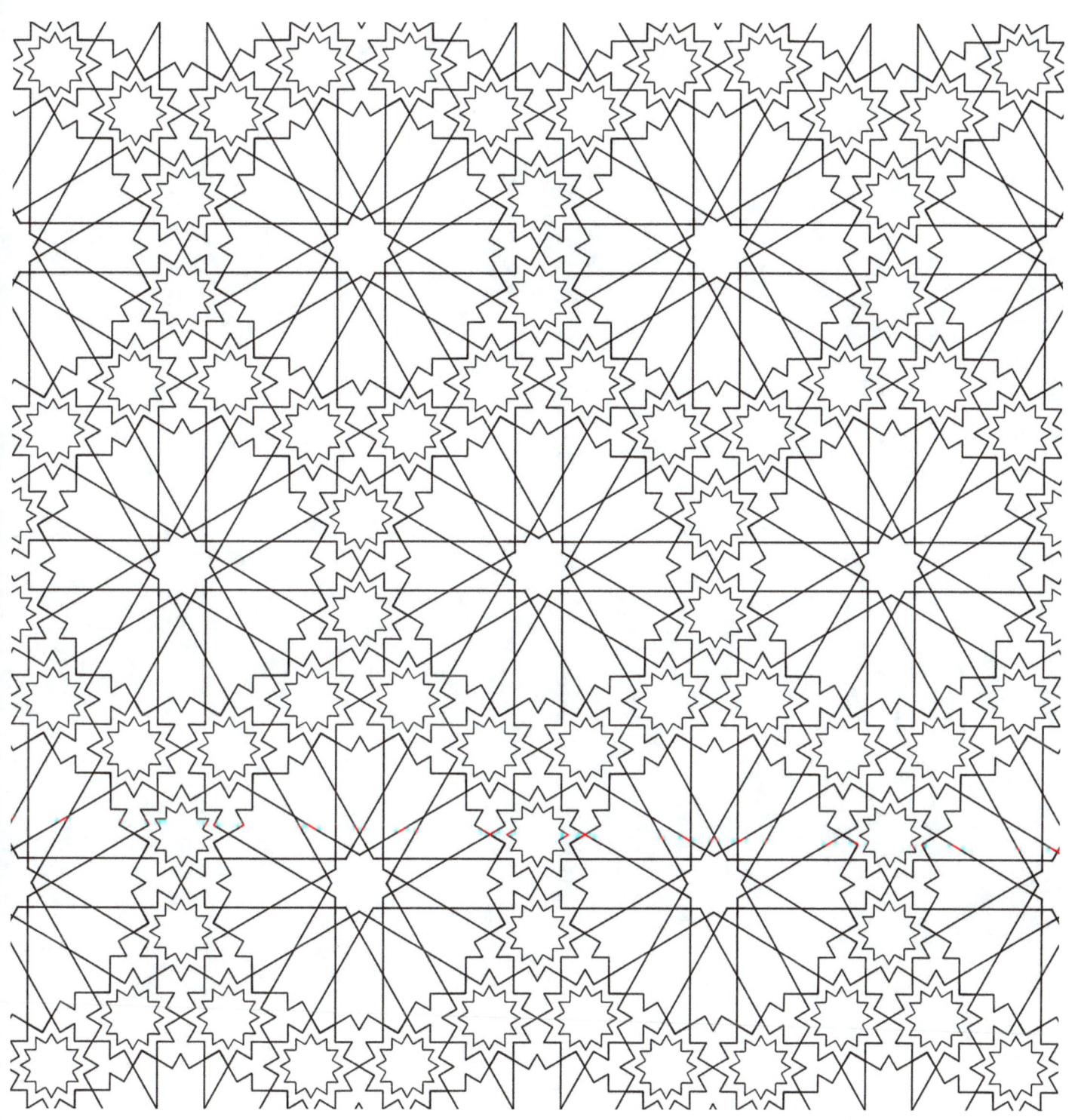

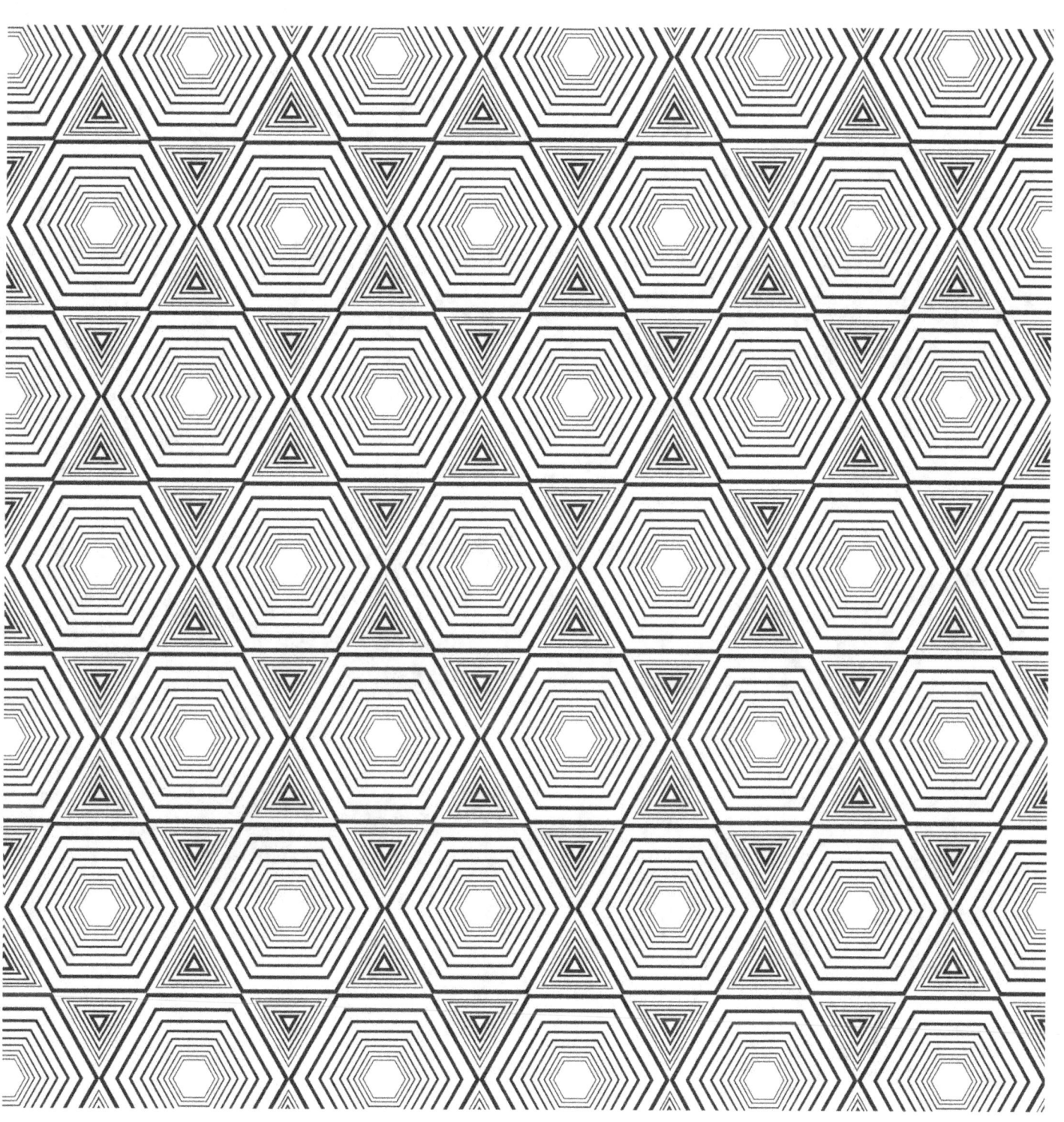